MEDIEVAL BRITAIN IN 100 FACTS

MATTHEW LEWIS

First published 2015

Amberley Publishing
The Hill, Stroud
Gloucestershire, GL5 4EP

www.amberley-books.com

British Library Cataloguing in Publication Data.
A catalogue record for this book is available from the British Library.

ISBN 978 1 4456 4734 0 (paperback)
ISBN 978 1 4456 4735 7 (ebook)

Typeset in 11pt on 13.5pt Sabon.
Typesetting and Origination by Amberley Publishing.
Printed in the UK.

THE FACTS

Introduction

The medieval period is typically viewed as a superstitious era of wrong thinking, populated by a majority of ignorant, dirty, smelly peasants ruled by a minority of rich, obnoxious, detached lords and nobles. In some parts this is accurate, but the true picture is much more complex. Fortunes within families both rich and poor waxed and waned and the state of learning moved ever forward.

Medieval society was in fact far more sophisticated than it is often perceived to be, and many misconceptions made by medieval scholars were based upon accumulated evidence and ancient teachings. Although now many of their theories have been disproved by modern science, they were the pinnacle of learning in their time.

The layers of society were far more nuanced than simply lords and peasants, a complexity fuelled by the emergence of a wealthy, literate, well-travelled merchant class. Religion was at the epicentre of medieval life for everyone, structuring the day and dominating all of their actions in an effort to earn a place in Heaven. Life was often short and sometimes brutal, but had to be endured. Hope lay in salvation and a good life was the only evidence one could rely on to earn eternal happiness.

There are many facts about the medieval era that have lodged in the collective consciousness so that we think we know things without knowing how we know them. Some of these things are true, some only tell part of the story and some are simply incorrect and can be disproved.

Contained herein are 100 facts, some true, some not

well known and some that will set the record straight. In their telling, we will take a whistle-stop tour of 500 years of British history, dipping in for glimpses of the lives our ancestors lived and hopefully enjoying the expedition into the past.

1. EDGAR II WAS THE LAST ANGLO SAXON KING OF ENGLAND

The Norman invasion of 1066 saw William the Bastard, Duke of Normandy, defeat Harold Godwinson, otherwise known as Harold II of England. The Battle of Hastings ended the Anglo-Saxon House of Wessex's grip on their kingdom. William the Conqueror thereby founded the Norman dynasty.

However, that's not quite the whole story. After Harold's death it was not William who was immediately proclaimed king. The Anglo-Saxon kings were appointed by the Witenagemot, a gathering of the senior nobles and ecclesiastical representatives which advised the King of England's various domains. Under the House of Wessex the kingdoms had been united and thus the Witenagemot had become a national body akin to a parliament. Succession was not necessarily hereditary and a king had to be appointed by the council's members. When Harold was slain, they did not simply turn to his vanquisher.

Edgar the Ætheling was around fifteen years of age in 1066. The title Ætheling denotes a member of Anglo-Saxon royalty who was considered at least a potential heir to the throne. Edgar was a great-grandson of Æthelred the Unready. Edgar's grandfather, Edmund Ironside, had lost his throne to the Viking Canute and Edgar's father, Edward the Exile, had lived in Eastern Europe for most of his life. Edgar and his parents, along with his two sisters, returned to England during the reign of Edward the Confessor and it is possible that the king intended to name Edgar's father his heir. However, Edward the Exile died within months of his return to England and Edgar was just a child, too young to assume power in the perilous last years of Edward the Confessor's rule. All of this is part of the reason why Edward never properly designated an heir.

When Edward died in January 1066 the Witenagemot elected Earl Godwin's son Harold, an experienced warrior and politician in his forties, to be king. It was not unusual for power to pass out of the direct male line of the House of Wessex when an heir was young and it was probably generally understood that Harold, the most powerful noble in the land, would be a steward for his lifetime, after which Edgar would be king. When Harold was killed at Hastings, the Witenagemot immediately elected and proclaimed Edgar, the last male heir of the House of Wessex, as Edgar II.

From that moment on, Edgar's life was an epic tale of rebellions and close calls. He constantly acted as figurehead for revolts against William I and William II. Eventually, Henry I married Edgar's niece and Edgar died in peace sometime after 1125. Quite how he gained the forgiveness of the harsh Norman kings so many times remains a mystery.

2. WILLIAM THE CONQUEROR'S CORONATION WAS A CHAOTIC AFFAIR

Following his victory at Hastings, Duke William of Normandy was crowned King of England at Westminster Abbey by Ealdred, Archbishop of York. Ealdred had supported Harold, then backed Edgar the Ætherling, but on Christmas Day 1066 found himself performing the sacred ceremony that would consecrate a Norman as king of Anglo-Saxon England.

William set an armed guard around the abbey in anticipation of trouble from the recently defeated indigenous population. Orderic Vitalis, a monk chronicler, was an eyewitness to the coronation and the chaos that broke out. William had both Norman and Anglo-Saxon nobility and churchmen within the abbey and alongside Ealdred stood Geoffrey, Bishop of Coutances. All was running smoothly as Ealdred lowered the crown onto William's head, but Orderic notes that the trouble that followed was 'at the prompting of the devil, who hates everything good'.

As the crown rested on the new monarch's head both Ealdred and Geoffrey asked the congregation whether they would accept William as their king. All of the congregation called out together that they would. The Anglo-Saxon nobility gathered within the abbey were desperate to demonstrate their commitment to William in order to preserve their position, but the Norman lords who had vanquished a nation would not be outdone. A less than angelic chorus rose to the abbey's ceiling as Orderic recalled how both sides 'gladly shouted out with one voice if not in one language'.

The harsh cacophony escaped the abbey and reached the ears of the Norman guards patrolling outside.

Orderic described their panicked reaction: 'Hearing the tumult of the joyful crowd in the church and the harsh accents of a foreign tongue, [the guards] imagined that some treachery was afoot.' Immediately convinced that things had gone wrong within the abbey the Norman guards began to set fire to the houses of London, the fire quickly spreading out of control through the timber buildings. The abbey doors flew open and Anglo-Saxon and Norman lords rushed out, some to fight the fire that was engulfing London and others to loot wherever they could in the havoc.

Inside the abbey only the clergymen remained with the king, who, Orderic noted, 'was trembling from head to foot' as the ceremony was concluded in an otherwise empty church. It was not an auspicious start for a new dynasty and Orderic Vitalis insists that as word spread of what the Normans had done in their panic, the disgusted English began to harbour a deep grudge against their new masters: a seed which would not take long to flourish into full-blown rebellion.

3. The Harrying of the North Left Deep Scars

In 1069 Sweyn Estrithsson, King of Denmark, landed near York to invade William the Conqueror's new kingdom. Sweyn offered support to Edgar the Ætherling in one of his many uprisings. The North was also a stronghold of the old Viking blood that lingered in England and did not want to accept Norman rule. William reacted swiftly and decisively against Sweyn, a man he had believed to be an ally.

The Norman army marched North and the king ordered his men to burn villages, crops and food stores as they went, murdering countless inhabitants. Orderic Vitalis, a monk with a Norman father and a Saxon mother, wrote in his otherwise pro-William chronicle of his disgust at the Harrying.

> The King stopped at nothing to hunt his enemies. He cut down many people and destroyed homes and land. Nowhere else had he shown such cruelty.
>
> To his shame he made no effort to control his fury and he punished the innocent with the guilty. He ordered that crops and herds, tools and food should be burned to ashes. More than 100,000 people perished of hunger.
>
> I have often praised William in this book, but I can say nothing good about this brutal slaughter. God will punish him.

As winter fell at the end of 1069, thousands of families starved or froze to death and there were rumours of cannibalism amongst those desperately trying to survive. William sent no aid. Simeon of Durham deplored the devastation, claiming that 'there was no village inhabited between York and Durham', an area covering sixty square miles. He lamented that 'it was horrible to observe, in houses, streets and roads, human corpses rotting ... for no-one survived to cover them with earth, all having perished by the sword and starvation, or left the land of their fathers because of hunger'.

It was a grim picture, but the Harrying of the North had the effect William desired. Sweyn did invade again, but always further south. The strong Norse connection in the North was broken forever, but the episode left deep scars on the region that would take many years to heal. The old Anglo-Saxon and Viking men of power were replaced by Norman lords, but Anglo-Saxon culture remained in place. The Normans, with William's blessing, built their castle walls high and thick to protect them from the people they sought to rule, but it would not be long before these stout fortresses were to provide the means to oppose the king rather than the people.

4. MEDIEVAL LAND DIVISIONS WERE INEXACT

During the medieval period it was vital for a king or lord to understand exactly how much land they controlled. This measure would determine tax revenue and influence the number of soldiers that could be mustered from an area. William the Conqueror's Domesday Book is a prime example of a new king needing to measure what he now owned.

The smallest unit of land measurement in use was a hide. During the Anglo-Saxon period the hide had been established as a parcel of land sufficient to support one peasant family. The precise dimensions of the piece of land could therefore vary to allow for terrain and even soil quality. It was only in the twelfth century that a hide was defined as covering 120 acres, an amount of land far beyond that required for one family and probably enough to support four or five families.

A hundred was a larger measurement of land made up of 100 hides. A legacy of the Anglo-Saxon administrative system retained well into the medieval era, every hundred held a monthly court at which anyone could bring civil or criminal proceedings to be heard by a judge, usually one of their peers in the community. Twice a year the sheriff would visit the court to sit as judge until local lords began to assume control of the hundred courts on their land. Any criminal offences committed within a hundred were the collective responsibility of those living within the hundred If the criminal was not found and brought before the court the entire community would have to pay a fine in reparation for the crime.

Hundreds were collected together into shires, each

of which could contain several hundreds and would come under the control in Anglo-Saxon times of an ealdorman and a sheriff. The Norman Conquest saw the arrival of the term 'county', which began to replace shire in official documentation, though shire remained in popular usage and still forms part of many county names today. Ealdormen were replaced by Norman lords, eventually becoming earldoms, but the post of sheriff was retained and has lasted to the present day.

Medieval understanding of land, its value and military potential were vital to the preservation of a kingdom and so a sophisticated system was developed under the Anglo-Saxons which was so efficient and effective that it was preserved, with only minor alterations, for centuries after the Norman Conquest. This apparently simple system of land and justice ensured that a lord and his king knew precisely how much money was due from a region and how many men it should provide in the event of war while also requiring the people to be responsible for justice within their own community.

5. The Domesday Book Quantified Only Part of England

Twenty years after his conquest of England, William I set upon the notion during the Christmas festivities of 1085 that he would compile a full list of his kingdom's resources and landowners. It was a unique undertaking in all of Europe and the like would not be seen again until national censuses began in the nineteenth century.

The Anglo-Saxon Chronicles record that the clerks went 'all over England into every shire [to] find out how many hides there were in the shire, what land and cattle the king had himself in the shire, what dues he ought to have in twelve months from the shire', complaining that 'so very narrowly did he have it investigated that there was no single hide nor yard of land, nor indeed ... one ox or cow or pig which was left out and not put down in his record, and these records were brought to him afterwards'. The writers of the Chronicle were naturally wary and bitter about a mechanism designed to permanently deprive them of their property.

The motivation for the survey was probably military. With the persistent threat of Viking invasion, William needed a clear idea of what his new country was worth in taxation and how much military support he could realistically expect from his nobility. The surveyors took with them a list of questions aimed at defining who had owned each piece of land during Edward the Confessor's reign and who owned it in 1086, how many hides made up the land and how many free and unfree people worked the land.

The swiftness with which the survey was compiled was astounding – it was presented to William at Old

Sarum before the end of 1086 – and the detail it records is minute. The volumes seem to have lacked an official name, only later becoming colloquially known as Great Domesday and Little Domesday. The Domesday Book was the Anglo-Saxon's disparaging name for the survey that would permanently and legally deprive them of land they had once owned and expose everything they still possessed to the invading king.

For all of its detail, the Domesday Book was far from a complete picture of the nation. London was not included in the survey, nor was Winchester. Bristol was not covered and neither were great swathes of the North, including Northumberland and Durham. After William the Conqueror's death in 1087 his son, William II, had no interest in completing the survey and it was abandoned.

Domesday was a triumph of medieval administration, harnessing the already complex Anglo-Saxon governmental structure. Feared as a tool of suppression, it was more likely designed simply as an information-gathering exercise. As impressive as it remains, it was a task that was left incomplete.

6. WILLIAM RUFUS WAS NOT A REDHEAD

On his death, William the Conqueror left his oldest son, Robert, the duchy of Normandy. The kingdom of England he bequeathed to his second surviving son, who became William II. This was perhaps a measure of the importance the Conqueror gave to his respective domains, though it may well also reflect the personalities of his sons.

William II is remembered by the nickname William Rufus and it is frequently asserted that he earned this epithet from his mop of flame-red hair. A contemporary description of the king by the chronicler William of Malmesbury sets the record straight on that front. He notes that William Rufus was

> 'well set; his complexion florid, his hair yellow; of open countenance; different coloured eyes, varying with certain glittering specks; of astonishing strength, though not very tall, and his belly rather projecting'.

It seems most likely that William earned the Rufus tag from the 'florid' complexion that William of Malmesbury describes and the king's legendary temper would certainly have turned his cheeks even redder when his blood was heated. The king was a famed soldier and inspired great loyalty in his men, to whom he was lavishly generous. On the other hand, the Church did not approve of much of William's character or actions. His love of tournaments and his generosity to his men cost money, which he obtained by keeping religious posts vacant so that he could enjoy the income. He kept the See of Canterbury empty for four years so that he could claim its income.

The rumours of homosexual relationships and constant blasphemous curses did not help the relationship. The chronicles noted that 'God's face!' and 'by the holy face of Lucca!' were amongst his favourite expletives. Ranulf Flambard rose to become William's most effective servant. William of Malmesbury wrote that he 'skinned the rich, ground down the poor, swept other men's inheritances into his net' in his pursuit of money for his master, but the criticism of the chroniclers, who were almost exclusively monks, is a symptom of William's success in administrative and martial affairs.

William was as famed for his short temper as for his martial prowess and irreligiousness. Over time the nickname Rufus has been misunderstood as referring to William's hair colour. Later portraits frequently show him with red hair, but William of Malmesbury's contemporary description gives the lie to this notion, confirming that he had blonde hair, whilst also pointing to the frequently enflamed colour in his cheeks as the real reason that he is remembered as William Rufus.

7. Unmaking a Deer Was an Important Hunting Ritual

Hunting for sport was a favourite pursuit of the Norman kings and became a vital part of British elite social life throughout the medieval period. It was, however, enwrapped by rituals that appear very pagan in nature.

Engaging in the hunt was not really about providing food for the rich. It was a social occasion that helped to establish status and rank. It also provided practise for the battlefield, honing riding skills and allowing practise with bow and arrow, spear and sword against moving targets. It became popular because men enjoyed it too, especially kings.

When a stag was killed in the hunt there was a very particular ritual that was performed which may seem bizarre, but which actually served to reinforce the defining of social rank provided by the act of hunting. The ritual was known as unmaking the deer, sometimes also referred to as breaking or undoing the animal. It was viewed as the climax of a day-long hunt and the fullest description of the process was written into the Boke of Seynt Albans in the fifteenth century.

The treatment of the dead stag was divided into three parts. Firstly, the undoing saw the stag's genitalia and some organs placed atop a pole called the *forchée*, which was carried before the procession home. The stag was then slit open from front to back along its stomach and across to each leg. The right hind hoof was removed and given to the highest status member of the hunt, man or woman, as a mark of their superiority. Next, the fleaning took place, skinning the stag and using the skin to protect the meat and collect the blood from the carcass. Finally, the body was brittled: cut into pieces to be ceremonially distributed. The pelvis was left at the kill site as a gift to the ravens. The left shoulder was given as payment to the forester who cared for the land on which the deer was killed.

The rear haunches were the prime cuts of the venison (a word derived from the French *venesoun*, meaning 'product of hunting') and were destined for the top table. The kidneys, small intestines, windpipe and collected blood of the stag were mixed with bread and fed to the hunting hounds while they were held on leashes by their masters so that they associated the reward with the hunt and with obedience.

The lesser parts of the body, including the offal and the umbles (the entrails) were fed to the lowest status members of the household. The term eating humble pie is believed to have derived from this demonstration of low social status. Part of the reason that hunting was so popular amongst the aristocracy of medieval Britain, and with kings in particular, is precisely because the rituals surrounding it clearly demonstrated their superiority to all those about them.

8. William II Was Shot While Hunting, but Was It an Accident?

On 2 August 1100 William II was in the New Forest indulging in one of his favourite pastimes: hunting with his closest friends and his younger brother Henry. The king had been unwell during the day, but as dusk fell he decided that he was well enough to ride out. During the hunt William was struck with an arrow and died. One of his best friends, Sir Walter Tyrell, Lord of Piox de Picardie, is traditionally accused of discharging the fatal arrow and has long come under suspicion for the deed.

The previous evening William Rufus is supposed to have given Walter a pair of arrows, telling him 'to the good archer, the good arrows'. During the hunt, Walter is supposed to have shot at a deer, but the arrow instead pierced the king's heart. It was one of the arrows gifted to Walter that was found lodged in William's chest.

Chronicles are less clear on the matter than the story that has passed into legends. The Peterborough Manuscript, contained within the Anglo-Saxon Chronicles, states only that 'king William was shot with an arrow in hunting by a man of his'. Geoffrey Gaimer claimed that 'we do not know who shot the king' while Gerald of Wales would assert that 'the King was shot by Ranulf of Aquis'. The tradition later grew that Walter Tyrell had shot the king, though Abbot Suger, a prominent French clergyman and statesman who knew Tyrell, insisted, 'I have often heard him, when he had nothing to fear nor to hope, solemnly swear that on the day in question he was not in the part of the forest where the king was hunting, nor ever saw him in the forest at all.' Suspicion lingers about Walter, in part because he fled immediately to France and never returned.

The reaction to William's death has caused further speculation that it was not, in fact, an accident at all. All of the lords in William's hunting party fled, returning to their lands to ensure their own security in the uncertainty that would follow. Walter Tyrell left for France immediately and never returned to England, though there is no evidence that he received any reward from any source that might incriminate him further. William's older brother, Robert, Duke of Normandy, who was returning from Crusade, might have expected to inherit the English crown, but instead Henry rushed from the New Forest to Winchester to secure the royal treasury and just three days later, on 5 August, he was crowned Henry I at Westminster Abbey. This unseemly haste has cast a shadow of suspicion over Henry's own potential involvement in his brother's death.

In the panic to secure their own positions, no one gave a thought for the old king. According to tradition, William's body lay where it had fallen in the New Forest until a charcoal burner by the name of Purkiss found the corpse and placed the king in his wagon, carrying the body to Winchester for burial. It remains a mystery precisely who shot the king, for none would wish to admit it. Whether it was an accident or murder also remains unknown.

9. Castle Tower Steps Are Usually a Clockwise Spiral

Castles were the great war machines of domination in the middle ages, immovable tanks imported with the Norman Conquest. They loomed over their new Anglo-Saxon subjects, casting a long, dark shadow. Castle design evolved as the purpose of the castle slowly moved from dominance to maintenance and eventually to provide comfortable accommodation.

Staircases were important to the design of castles and the success of just two methods of climbing levels can be seen in the ruins that sit throughout Britain today. Many castles, particularly those with a Norman keep, have a main entrance that sits significantly above ground level. Many have a broad, straight stone staircase leading up to them today, but these are later additions that reflect the relaxing of the castle's military footing. At the height of the castle's power these doors would have been accessed by wooden ladders. At night or when the castle came under threat these ladders could be withdrawn to make the keep all but inaccessible to attackers.

Even if an attacking force breached a castle's outer defences, the moat, the murder holes of the gatehouse and the portcullis, even the stairs within the towers were set up with defence in mind. Look at almost any spiral staircase within a castle and it will turn in a clockwise spiral. These staircases are constructed using keyhole-shaped slabs of stone with the circular narrow ends placed one atop another to form a central column and the broader end built into the wall. By staggering the slabs as they are laid a spiral staircase is formed.

The reason the staircases almost exclusively turned

in a clockwise direction is because that arrangement favoured the defender coming from above with a sword in his right hand against an attacker coming from below using his right hand. The attacker was forced to expose more of his body to the defender in order to use his sword. Very little in castle design was accidental.

10. A Young Boy Had to Tell Henry I His Son Was Dead

Following William II's death and Henry I's hasty coronation, the new king's older brother Robert, Duke of Normandy, invaded to dispute Henry's claim. Robert was defeated and returned to his own lands, but in retaliation Henry I invaded Normandy in 1105, winning a decisive victory a year later.

Henry I was keen to return to England after defeating and imprisoning his older brother. He was now the undisputed ruler of England and Normandy. The King of France had even recognised Henry's son and heir 'William' as the next Duke of Normandy. It was now, at the very height of his power, that fate dealt a cruel blow.

William Adelin (a Norman version of Ætheling adopted for Henry's son) was seventeen years old and Henry's only legitimate son. The hopes of the Anglo-Norman dynasty rested upon his young shoulders. As the royal party prepared to leave from Barfleur a ship's captain called Thomas Fitzstephen approached the king and offered the services of his stunning new ship, the fastest vessel around, named the *White Ship*. Thomas recalled that his grandfather had sailed Henry's father, William the Conqueror, across the Channel in 1066.

Henry was pleased, but said that his ship was already prepared. Instead, he offered to let Thomas take his son William and two of his illegitimate children, Robert and Matilda, along with Henry's party of young nobles in his new vessel. Delighted, Thomas made preparations to sail. William and his friends, around 300 in total, poured onto the ship. So many embarked that some decided to return to land. Amongst them was Henry's favourite nephew, Stephen of Blois, who claimed that a case of diarrhoea meant that he could no longer make the crossing. It was to prove a fateful decision for the future King Stephen.

At around midnight on 25 November 1120 the *White Ship* cast off, its unruly young occupants already drunk or still drinking, trying to catch up to the king's ship. The boat suddenly hit a large rock, tearing a hole in the port side. As the passengers panicked, the *White Ship* listed and was swallowed up from the night by the black seas. Although it was calm, only two men survived, clinging to the mast.

One account tells of William's escape in a small boat, but when he heard his sister Matilda calling for help he turned back to save her only for his little craft to be swamped by others trying to climb aboard, sinking to the depths with Henry's heir. Another explains how the ship's captain, Thomas, bobbed to the surface and asked what had become of William. When he was told, he sighed that there was no point in him trying to survive only to be killed by the king and, with that, he disappeared beneath the water.

During the night one of the survivors, Geoffrey of Laigle, could hold on no longer and was lost, leaving only a butcher named Berold to be saved with the morning light. As news reached England of the disaster none wanted to tell Henry. In the end a small boy was pushed before the grumpy king to break the worst news of his life.

11. Christ and His Saints Were Asleep

The *White Ship* disaster had left Henry I without a son. He did, however, have a legitimate daughter, Matilda. Born in 1102, Matilda had been married to Henry V, Holy Roman Emperor, in 1114 until his death in 1125. Three years later her father arranged a marriage to Geoffrey, Count of Anjou. Unhappy at being forced into a union with a mere count, Matilda kept her imperial title. Henry I ordered all of his nobles to pledge fealty to Matilda, but on his death in 1135 his plans came to nothing.

Matilda was in France with her husband and made no urgent efforts to return home. There were several reasons why the English aristocracy viewed her with caution and suspicion. That Matilda was a woman was the first bar to her succession. Although there was no law against female succession, men of power found the notion of bending the knee to a lady uncomfortable. Equally out of kilter was the thought of a woman exercising the power of a man. To do so was, well, unwomanly.

Gender was not Matilda's only problem. Her husband was an Angevin, a hated enemy of the Normans and now the English. The thought of him acting as king (because he was, after all, her husband) terrified them. Then there was the issue of Matilda's personality. Abrupt, autocratic, arrogant and aloof, she possessed many of the qualities that might make a good king. In a woman, though, they instilled horror.

When Stephen of Blois, the son of Henry I's sister, dashed to claim the crown, the nobles saw a way out of their problems. Stephen was a grandson of William the Conqueror and had been a favourite of Henry I. When he claimed that his uncle had undergone a change of heart at the last and nominated Stephen as his heir, the nobility were only too happy to accept the tale.

England was plunged into nineteen years of savage civil war, known as the Anarchy, as Stephen and Matilda fought bitterly for the crown. Stephen was, it seems, a very nice man, perhaps too nice to make a good king. Having captured Matilda once, he released her. When her son, Henry, invaded and Stephen defeated him, the king paid his enemy's soldiers wages when Henry could not afford to. Matilda refused to give in. The Anglo-Saxon Chronicle lamented the period, complaining that 'wherever cultivation was done, the ground produced no corn, because the land was all ruined by such doings, and they said openly that Christ and his saints were asleep. Such things too much for us to describe, we suffered nineteen years for our sins'.

Finally, Stephen conceded that it had to end. The Treaty of Winchester in 1153 provided for Stephen to remain as king for the rest of his life and for Matilda's son Henry to succeed. A year later Stephen was dead and Henry II began a new dynasty, the Plantagenets, who would rule England for the remainder of the medieval period.

12. PRESERVING FOOD PREVENTED FAMINE

Before proper refrigeration medieval society found ways to preserve their food effectively and efficiently. The notion that most meat was rotten and spiced to disguise the taste is simply incorrect. Those who could afford spices would have ensured a supply of preserved foods that were far from rotten. Preserved food protected people against periods of drought and famine and were vital in times of war. Methods of preservation also aided those who had to transport food over great distances, such as soldiers when at sea and on campaign and merchants, sailors and pilgrims making long journeys. Eating foods out of season is not such a new phenomenon.

Salt played a crucial role in the preservation of food. It aided in other methods but salting was a preservation technique in its own right. Even without an understanding of the microbial impact of moisture on decomposition, medieval people could not fail to notice that food left outside in the damp and warm rotted, reeked and hummed with flies. Salt drew the moisture out of meat and fish – and occasionally vegetables – allowing it to last for years. The least-effective method of salt preservation was soaking in brine, which could still preserve meat for up to two years.

For long-term preservation meat was sliced into thin strips and salt was pressed into it. The salted meat was then stored in barrels, each piece surrounded completely by salt. This method could keep meat edible for up to four years, though it meant that care had to be taken when using the meat. Once removed from its barrel the meat would have to be soaked in fresh water, perhaps several times, to remove as much salt as possible before cooking. Many medieval recipes were designed to compensate for the salty nature of the meat or fish, using ingredients to either counteract or complement the salty taste.

Drying food was another important method used to preserve it. Salting frequently played a role in drying and the principle was similar: the removal of moisture was crucial to the long term preservation of food. Meat could be dried outside or within an enclosed area at most times of the year and grain could also be dried to lengthen its life. Smoking was similar to drying, but used the heat of fires to speed the drying process. The choice of fuel could have an impact on the flavour of the meat too, improving it for later consumption. Confits were potted meats, salted and cooked in their own fat, cooled in their own fat and then sealed in airtight containers.

Pickling vegetables was a popular method of preservation, involving soaking in water or brine, perhaps with herbs or vinegar to affect the flavour. Fruit would usually be preserved in honey, a method in use for centuries by the Middle Ages. More affluent households could even afford sugar to boil the fruit in.

This resourcefulness preserved life as well as food for a medieval family.

13. HENRY I HOLDS THE RECORD FOR ILLEGITIMATE CHILDREN

Henry I, youngest son of William the Conqueror, was nicknamed Beauclerc – 'good cleric' – possibly because of his education. As the youngest son of a duke he was perhaps intended for the Church. If he was, that life seems unsuitable for a man who, at his death, would set a record as yet unbeaten throughout history for the number of illegitimate children fathered by a King of England.

When he ascended to his brother's throne in 1100 Henry already had several illegitimate children. Within three months of becoming king in his early thirties he married Matilda, daughter of Malcolm III of Scotland. Matilda's mother had been a princess of the Anglo-Saxon House of Wessex and Henry saw that in his attempt to develop stability there would be an advantage of seeming to be sympathetic to the Anglo-Saxon majority. His desire for peace, however, did not stop his eyes from wandering.

Described by William of Malmesbury as 'of middle stature, his hair was black, but scanty near the forehead, his eyes mildly bright, his chest brawny, his body well fleshed', his unspectacular physical appearance was certainly no hindrance. Henry became a serial adulterer and by his death in 1135 in his mid-sixties he had fathered at least twenty illegitimate sons and daughters. Some estimates put the number even higher.

Amongst those illegitimate children were several persons of note. Reginald became Earl of Cornwall. One Matilda married Rotrou, Count of Perche, and became his countess, but would die aboard the *White Ship* in 1120. Another Matilda was wedded to Conan

III, Duke of Brittany, becoming duchess of the region. A third Matilda (a popular Norman name that had been that of Henry's mother, but which was also his wife's name) became Abbess of the Church of Notre-Dame in Montvilliers. Sybilla married Alexander I, King of Scotland and became a queen; though she died childless, Alexander founded a priory in her memory on Kenmore in Loch Tay as a sign of his devotion and affection.

Perhaps the most famous of Henry's illegitimate children was his firstborn, Robert, who would become Earl of Gloucester and the leading military supporter of his legitimate half-sister, the Empress Matilda. Robert was a devoted servant to his half-sister and died trying to win the throne of England for her. The *Gesta Stephani*, a contemporary chronicle by an unknown writer which is full of important detail about the period, claims that Robert was offered the throne after his father's death but refused to accept, insisting that it belonged to his sister, the empress, and her infant son, the future Henry II.

Henry I's record remains unbeaten, even by the prodigious efforts of Charles II. Several of his natural children led extraordinary lives, but it was Henry's failure to leave a surviving, legitimate male heir that would scar England for decades to come.

14. People in Medieval Times Had a Cleanliness Regime

The importance of bathing was well understood and formed a part of several treatises. The fourteenth-century *Regimen Sanitatis* recognized that 'the bath cleans the external body parts of dirt left behind from exercise on the outside of the body'. By the fifteenth century John Russell was laying out detailed advice for servants who were preparing a bath for their master. King John took a bath only once every three weeks, but Edward IV paid a barber a pitcher of wine and two loaves of bread every Saturday to shave him and wash his head, legs and feet. Manuals to improve manners frequently referred to the need to wash hands and faces on a daily basis and keep fingernails clean.

While private bathing was the reserve of the wealthy, public bathhouses could be found in towns around Britain. Monasteries frequently had water piped in and prescribed bathing regimes for the brotherhood – though this might stipulate just four baths a year! It is unclear whether this was a prescribed minimum or a restrictive maximum. Images of bathing can be found in medieval manuscripts, created in monasteries, which suggests that it was a commonplace business worthy of inclusion by the monks.

The bathing habits of those outside the towns are less easy to discern, but they would surely have appreciated the benefits – to both health and personal odour – of cleaning away the dirt and sweat of a day's work in the fields. The growing problem of finding affordable firewood to heat water for bathing meant full baths might have become a luxury enjoyed less frequently, with families forced to share water.

15. Empress Matilda Escaped Oxford Castle in Camouflage

England was in the grip of the Anarchy as King Stephen and Empress Matilda fought bitterly for the crown. The fortunes of the civil war fluctuated, as neither side was able to hold on to the upper hand for long. In the winter of 1142 Empress Matilda was trapped, besieged by the forces of Stephen within the walls of Oxford Castle.

Matilda was establishing Oxford as a centre of her operations when her cousin Stephen launched a lightening attack on the town. Matilda was trapped within the castle with a small garrison and no food. Unprepared to withstand the siege, Matilda knew that they could not last out for long, but she had no intention of falling into Stephen's hands.

It was December and the winter was harsh. Snow lay on the ground and the part of the River Thames that ran past the castle, now known as Castle Mill Stream, was frozen solid. Matilda, or someone close to her within the castle, came up with an idea that kept her free and prolonged the bitter civil war.

Matilda and a handful of men climbed down from St George's Tower dressed all in white. Using the cover of the snow they walked across the river and slipped away from the besieging force. It is believed that Matilda walked all the way to Abingdon to secure her freedom. Camouflage and ingenuity kept Matilda at large and kept the civil war of the Anarchy going for another decade.

16. GEOFFREY OF MONMOUTH FORETOLD THE BATTLE OF BOSWORTH

During the first half of the twelfth century a Welsh cleric by the name of Geoffrey of Monmouth pioneered the written telling of the history of Britain. It may not have been the kind of history that we would recognise today, but his works were popular for hundreds of years and helped to mould the idealistic version of King Arthur that blossomed throughout the medieval era. In one passage he seems to foretell the struggle that would end the period.

Geoffrey recounted the story of Vortigern, King of the Britons, who was forced from power by Saxons that he had invited into his kingdom as friends. The king fled into Snowdonia and found a spot at Dinas Emrys upon which he began to build a defensive tower. Each night, the day's work was undone and left in a pile of rubble. Wise men told the king that he must shed the blood of a child without a father to remove the curse. The boy that was found was named Merlin, but he challenged the wise men, instructing Vortingern's men to dig further into the foundation.

Deep in the earth, they uncovered two sleeping dragons, one white and one red, which immediately rose up and began a fierce battle. The white dragon had the upper hand to begin with but was eventually forced to flee by the red. Vortigern asked what the discovery and battle meant and Merlin told the king that the white dragon represented the Saxons, who had invaded the land of the red dragon, who was the Britons. Although the white dragon would hold sway for a time, the red would rise again and chase him out.

When Geoffrey was writing, Wales was under the

control of Henry I, the Norman king. After Henry's death there was bitter fighting in Wales and Geoffrey perhaps saw an opportunity to remind Wales of its proud heritage as the last bastion of true Briton. His tales of King Arthur and prophecies of red dragons rising to drive out invaders were timely and would have appealed to his audiences.

It was no accident that when Henry Tudor invaded in 1485, he landed in Wales and marched north along the coast behind his banner, the red dragon. He was drawing on this latent but powerful mythology to offer himself as a new Merlin, come to lead the nation to freedom. In common with Merlin, Henry was a man without a father. Edmund Tudor had died before Henry's birth. The red dragon took the field at Bosworth for the true people of Albion and drove out the white dragon, or at least the white rose of the House of York.

Henry Tudor named his first son Arthur in 1486, completing the prophecy of the once and future king, led to power by the fatherless boy for the glory of the British people. The harnessing of centuries of prophecy helped to carry Henry Tudor to power.

17. THE ONLY ENGLISH POPE SAVED ROME

Nicholas Breakspear was born around the turn of the twelfth century in St Albans, already a religious centre of great importance. When he was refused entry to a local monastery as a young boy Nicholas left for France and became a canon at St Rufus in Avignon, where he was eventually abbot, gaining a reputation for strict discipline. Eloquence and good looks brought him to the attention of Rome, where Pope Eugenius held the English people in high regard.

In 1152 Nicholas was despatched to Scandinavia as papal legate to reform the church in the region. Two years later Nicholas returned to Rome having achieved complete and unprecedented success. He established the archiepiscopal see at Trondheim in Norway, his assistance to the region extending to its civil administration. One contemporary chronicler noted that no foreigner had earned as much public respect and adulation as Nicholas Breakspear.

The Englishman received a warm welcome on his return to Rome, and when Pope Anastasius IV died on 2 December 1154 Nicholas was unanimously elected as his replacement the following day. Taking the name Adrian IV, there were very compelling reasons for Breakspear's selection. Rome and the Papacy had been under siege for years and had endured successive weak popes; King William of Sicily was threatening war; Frederick Barbarossa had been elected king of Germany and wanted to be enthroned as Holy Roman Emperor. A tough, decisive man was needed.

The most pressing issue was the hostile occupation of Rome by Arnold of Brescia. Adrian found himself confined to St Peter's after his enthronement and his first move was to ask Arnold to leave Rome. It must have come as no surprise when he was ignored. In a make-or-break step, within weeks of becoming Pope, Adrian issued an interdict against the whole of Rome. All church services were suspended. No masses. No marriages. No bells filling the streets of Rome. Baptism of newborns and absolution for the dying continued, but as Easter grew closer the city panicked. Adrian's brinkmanship worked and the people drove Arnold out.

Frederick Barbarossa was the next problem to be tackled. He was heading south through Italy with a large army. In June, Adrian rode north to meet him. Riding into camp, tradition required the emperor to lead the pope's horse by the bridle, help him dismount, see the pope enthroned and kiss his feet. The pope would then rise and give the emperor the kiss of peace. Frederick did not lead in Adrian's horse or help him dismount. He did kiss Adrian's feet, but the pope did not give the kiss of peace, withholding it until the affront was corrected. Two days later, the meeting was repeated and Frederick played his part in full.

The only Englishman ever to sit upon the papal throne was a strong, steadying hand when the Papacy needed it most. Refusing to back down when threatened was precisely what was required, and precisely what Nicholas Breakspear provided.

18. The Bishop's Brothels Made Him Rich

During the medieval period brothels existed throughout the cities of Britain. The most famous red-light district was in Southwark in London. Interestingly, this area came under the rent control of the Bishop of Winchester.

In the early twelfth century Henry I granted a parcel of land on the south bank of the Thames, opposite the City of London, to the Priory of Bermondsey. In 1149 the priory sold the land to Henry of Blois, Bishop of Winchester and younger brother of King Stephen. The Bishop wanted a residence close to London for his governmental business. The area became known as the Liberty of Winchester and adopted the nickname of the Liberty of the Clink, a name derived from the Bishop's prison, which was known as the Clink.

In 1161 Henry II granted Bishop Henry the power to licence brothels and prostitutes to operate within the Liberty. The area sat outside the jurisdiction of both London and of the county of Sussex in which it nominally sat. This meant that activities frowned upon in other areas could be considered legal within the Liberty. Brothels began to grow up in Bankside, an area in the Liberty that ran along the south bank of the Thames. These were colloquially known as 'stews' as many also operated as bathhouses, full of steam.

The prostitutes of Bankside became known as Winchester Geese and a dose of goosebumps became a euphemism for contracting venereal disease. The bishops of Winchester grew rich from rents, shares in the profits of brothels and the fines imposed on prostitutes too. In spite of this relationship, the prostitutes were reputedly buried in a mass graveyard on unconsecrated ground along with other social outcasts, as their trade, despite being sanctioned by and to the profit of the bishop, was considered immoral. Crossbones, as the graveyard was named, remains today on Redcross Way, not far from the high street. It has been suggested that up to 15,000 bodies have been buried there.

The stews of Bankside remained in operation until 13 April 1546 when Henry VIII outlawed all brothels within the kingdom on the grounds that they spread disease. Henry VII had closed them for a year in 1504 amidst fears of the spreading of syphilis and Henry VIII had tried to close them in 1535 before finally succeeding a decade later.

It is a great irony of medieval attitude that a bishop could license and profit from brothels whilst denying the women who worked in them a Christian burial. The Church would preach from the pulpit the evils of visiting the establishments that they permitted to exist and from which they made vast amounts of money.

19. DID HENRY II REALLY ORDER THOMAS BECKET'S DEATH?

Thomas Becket, Archbishop of Canterbury, was one of the most revered saints in England until the Reformation. He was famously attacked and killed within Canterbury Cathedral on 29 December 1170 by four knights who believed that they were following the king's instructions. Doubt has long been cast upon the traditional interpretation of the outburst by Henry II that led to this disastrous but defining point in English history.

Thomas Becket was born in Cheapside, London, to Gilbert and Matilda Beket. Gilbert was a prospering London merchant of Norman descent whose connections meant that Becket was well educated and exposed to noble pastimes such as hunting. Eventually, Becket secured a position working for Theobald of Bec, Archbishop of Canterbury. Becket's success serving the Archbishop led to his recommendation to the king as Lord Chancellor, effectively the head of the king's government, in 1155 when the post became vacant.

Becket proved to be a loyal and effective servant to Henry II, ensuring that royal rights were exercised and that revenue flowed to the crown from wherever it might be sourced. When Theobald of Bec died in 1161 Becket was nominated as his successor, finally being appointed in mid-1162. Henry was seeking to shackle the Church, loosen its ties to Rome and gain more control over its substantial income. It made perfect sense to install a man who, by now, was not only a loyal and effective minister but also a close personal friend, trusted enough by Henry to have the king's son and heir placed within his household. Together, they would harness the power of the Church.

Henry's illusion did not last long. Becket seems to have felt the weight of his archbishop's mitre heavily upon his conscience and almost overnight he underwent a transformation from shrewd, ruthless political animal to ardent protector of the Church in England as its leading prelate. By 1163 Henry and Becket were at odds when the king demanded a traditional gift to local sheriffs should in future be paid to the crown as an obligation. Thomas openly opposed the move in council, though it was precisely the kind of thing he had done as chancellor and the very reason he had been made archbishop. Thomas won the argument and Henry was furious.

For seven years Becket was in exile, pursued and harried across Europe by Henry's agents. Finally, in 1170 Pope Alexander III tried to impose a reconciliation and Henry agreed to allow Becket to return to England. Thomas began to excommunicate several of his opponents and Henry was outraged once more. The traditional words accredited to him during his outburst are 'Will no one rid me of this turbulent priest?', though chronicler and eyewitness to Becket's death, Edward Grim, recorded them as 'What miserable drones and traitors have I nourished and promoted in my household, who allow their lord to be treated with such shameful contempt by a low-born cleric?'

Four knights took the words for a royal command. They rode to Canterbury and despatched the 'low-born cleric'. If they expected their master's thanks for the act, they were sorely disappointed.

20. Thomas Becket's Brains Were Spilled on the Floor of Canterbury Cathedral

Hugh de Morville, William de Tracy, Reginald FitzUrse and Richard le Bret joined together in 1170 to see a deed done that they must have believed their king had ordered and which they, reluctantly or to garner favour, took upon themselves. On 29 December 1170 they entered Canterbury Cathedral with swords drawn to commit an act, the infamy of which would forever define their king's reign.

The four who rode to Canterbury were no mere knights, but powerful barons. Hugh is often considered to have been the leader of the group. William was the senior noble and could trace his descent from Godgifu, sister of Edward the Confessor, and his grandfather was an illegitimate son of Henry I. Reginald could also claim royal descent, his maternal grandmother being described variously as niece or illegitimate daughter of Henry I. Richard was probably the youngest and lowest ranking member of the group.

Around three o'clock in the afternoon of 29 December the company entered the palace to demand an audience with the archbishop. The barons accused Becket of misuse of his powers; Becket denied all. Tempers became frayed and voices rose, attracting more of those about the cathedral. Reginald lost his temper and declared Becket to be outside the king's protection, ordering all of the household to leave the room. No one moved. Reginald instead instructed the monks to ensure Becket did not escape whilst arresting two knights present. The four left with the knights in custody.

Out in the courtyard the four knights had the gates

opened and a small royal force flooded in, the gates securely shut behind them. They were taking control of the cathedral grounds. Two servants shut and bolted the hall door, so a small detachment rounded the cathedral, breaking in and reopening the doors. Becket was encouraged to the cathedral using a connecting passage where the monks, who had begun Vespers, began to bar the doors, only for Becket to order them to stop.

Moments later the four burst in, demanding to know where the traitor was. Becket called back, 'Here I am. No traitor to the king, but a priest of God. What do you want?' The knights tried to seize him but the archbishop resisted them. In the growing commotion a blow was struck, probably by Reginald. As Hugh kept the growing crowd back the other three fell upon the archbishop. Edward Grim, who had held Becket back from the knights, thrust out an arm, trying to stop the first blow. The sword sliced across Becket's head and cut into Grim's arm. William and Richard joined in the attack and Becket fell onto his face before the altar.

Richard delivered the final blow, bringing his weapon down so hard that it removed the crown of Becket's head and shattered the blade on the stone floor. The subdeacon, Hugh of Horsea, pushed his sword into the open skull and spilled the archbishop's blood and brains across the floor. The spilling of an archbishop's brains within the nation's leading cathedral was a dark moment with deep consequences, yet it was no knight who did the deed, but a cleric.

21. Pottage Was the Staple Food for the Majority

Pottage is a thick stew or soup that formed the basis of the medieval diet for all but the rich. It was a versatile dish, mainly because it had to be. Food was a scarce resource for many and they were forced to make the best of what they could gather.

The word pottage is derived from Old French, meaning the contents of a pot – and that is precisely what the dish was. For most peasants, meat was a rare luxury. If they possessed an animal it was far more valuable for the milk or eggs it might produce than simply for meat. Tenants would frequently be required to turn over a percentage of anything that they grew to the lord of the manor and so whatever they could nurture became even more precious.

Foraging played a vital role in the medieval diet. Strict rules governed what animals might be hunted – for example, killing a deer was poaching, but a hedgehog was fair game. Knowing what plants could be eaten was also a vital part of medieval survival. Understanding the properties and benefits of plant life, both for eating and treating ailments, meant that medieval peasants in Britain would have found the skills shown in a modern survival TV programme a walk in the park.

A typical peasant's home would have consisted of one room, with a central hearth providing the only available heat, light and cooking facility. A cooking pot would usually hang above the fire and into that would go whatever was available to eat from their crop, hunting and foraging. A typical pottage recipe began with a base of stock or water, to which was added any grain, beans or split peas available. Cabbage was a staple crop that might form the core of a pottage dish. Leeks, onions and carrots might be added if they could be found and additional flavouring depended upon herbs that could be grown or foraged. Rosemary, thyme, parsley and sage would improve the pot if they were available.

It would not be unusual for a pot to sit over a fire for days or weeks, being added to each day as supplies allowed. Meat might be a very occasional luxury to add protein to an otherwise lean meal. Research suggests that medieval peasants typically ate around 4-5,000 calories per day, double the recommended intake today, to allow them to sustain their physically demanding existence. Food was fuel and flavour a luxury – desirable but not a requirement. Eating enough to provide energy for the next day's hard labour was the priority and pottage was an affordable way to achieve it with whatever was available.

22. Eleanor of Aquitaine Spent Sixteen Years Imprisoned by Her Husband

Eleanor of Aquitaine was born around 1122, the oldest child of William, Duke of Aquitaine. Her brother's death in 1130 made her heir to one of the richest, most cultured regions of France, and therefore the most eligible bride in Europe. When her father died in 1137, she came into her inheritance and became the focus of attention at the highest level.

William died on Good Friday, 9 April 1137. On 25 July Eleanor was married to the son and heir of Louis VI of France, who became Louis VII just a week later. Although they had two daughters, no son arrived and Louis turned out to be too pious and distant for the more sophisticated Eleanor, who soon became bored by her husband.

Excitement presented itself in 1146 when Eleanor's uncle, Prince Raymond of Antioch, issued a call for help from the Holy Land. Eleanor took the cross and accompanied her husband on a crusade that proved a dismal failure and contributed to the end of Eleanor and Louis's marriage. The couple were divorced in 1152.

Within two months Eleanor had remarried. Henry of Anjou was ten years her junior, an opponent of Louis and keen to get his hands on the famously beautiful and intelligent Eleanor, who also happened to bring with her one of Europe's richest inheritances. Two years later Henry brought an end to the Anarchy when he succeeded King Stephen as Henry II. In her early thirties, Eleanor was a queen for a second time. For twenty years the couple lived in apparent happiness, having five sons and three daughters.

In 1173 all sign of unity between the royal couple vanished. Their oldest son, known as Young Henry, rebelled against his father's firm grip on power, insisting that he wanted more control for himself. He involved two of his younger brothers, Geoffrey and Richard, and his mother offered him support too. When the revolt failed, Eleanor was arrested and imprisoned.

For the next sixteen years the queen remained a prisoner of her husband. Allowed to appear on state occasions, her detention did grow more comfortable and less restrictive as the years passed. It is suggested that Henry wanted her to divorce him but that she refused. She did not enjoy her freedom again until 1189 when her husband died. Eleanor's favourite son, Richard, succeeded his father as Richard I and ordered his mother released immediately. In her mid-sixties, she resumed an active role in government, acting as regent when Richard left on Crusade and helping to arrange his ransom and release when he was captured.

With her youngest son John's succession in 1199, Eleanor effectively retired from English affairs. She moved back to Aquitaine and focused her attention there, living into her early eighties, dying on 1 April 1204. Eleanor was a fascinating woman: beautiful, clever and powerful in her own right. She refused to be ruled by her husband but was buried next to him, perhaps so that they could enjoy tormenting each other for eternity.

23. Henry II's Penance Defined His Reign

Within three years of his murder at Canterbury, Thomas Becket had been made a saint and a martyr for the church's liberty. Miracles of healing were reported on the spot where he had fallen. Henry II had been forced to accept a degree of responsibility, Louis VII of France, William, King of Scotland, and Count Philip of Flanders were invading his vast empire in alliance with his own sons. Henry was stained, perhaps cursed, by the murder. He needed to fix the problem.

When the king landed at Southampton on his return to England in July 1174 he hurried to Canterbury. As soon as the cathedral came into sight Henry dismounted and walked the rest of the way barefooted. Entering the church, he prostrated himself before the shrine that had grown about the murder site, spending the whole day and night in prayer and fasting before the shrine to his old friend and great enemy.

In the morning, lest any should believe that he was acting only for show, Henry gathered the monks, presented each with a scourge – a whip used to flagellate in the name of religious devotion – barred his back and ordered the monks to whip him. The next day Henry received absolution for his part in the affair and was reconciled to the Church. In an age conscious of signs from God, the news that arrived shortly after of a great victory against the Scots, achieved on the very day Henry received his absolution, was viewed as confirmation that God and St Thomas had forgiven the English king.

Henry's motives for his act of very public penance were probably not as simple as a need for spiritual absolution. His foreign rivals were against him and even his own sons were trying to force him from his throne. Many in the country believed Henry was cursed for his part in Becket's death. Dangerously, this made him a fair target for overthrow by foreign rulers, who could claim that they did God's work.

If he was going to keep his empire and regain the upper hand Henry had to be seen to have God back on his side. No medieval monarch could rule for long if the perception of divine appointment and favour did not surround them. Becket's shrine was already attracting stories of miracles and a cult was growing around the murdered archbishop. Henry saw a new use for his old friend and set to work harnessing that focus to repair his own faltering image. Those two days of penance and reconciliation defined the remainder of Henry's rule, as God appeared to shine upon him favourably again. The devout penitence of a mighty king also ensured St Thomas Becket's place in legend.

24. THE EXCHEQUER WAS A TALLY BOARD FOR WORKING OUT WHAT WAS OWED TO THE KING

The treatise *Dialogue Concerning the Exchequer* was compiled in 1176 by the royal treasurer Richard FitzNigel to describe the functioning of the financial accounting system in England. It is not known precisely when the Exchequer was first established, but following the Anarchy Henry II was presented with the problem of rebuilding shattered institutions.

The Exchequer was, in its early days, a biannual event rather than a department of government. Sheriffs were required to attend at the Exchequer twice a year to deliver the income that was due to the crown from the lands that they were responsible for managing. It was a tense, confrontational auditing exercise that left little room for error or abuse.

The barons who oversaw the Exchequer were frequently joined by senior officials, such as the chancellor, though that position was not directly related to finance as the Chancellor of the Exchequer is today. The justiciar was President of the Board and in charge of proceedings. Along one side of the table sat clerks recording entries and along the other were more clerks tallying the counters. When the sheriff, facing this intimidating array of officials, had provided accounts for crown lands within his shire, he was also required to give details of debts owed to the crown by private individuals.

The name Exchequer originates from a large ten-foot-by-five-foot cloth in a chequered pattern that was laid across a table. The name may have derived from the cloth's resemblance to a chessboard, the French word for which is *echiquier*. The cloth was designed to offer a visible representation of the money that was owed and paid in. Counters were placed on the chequered cloth and moved about to represent the income and to provide a visual aid to balancing the accounts.

The final result of the audit of each sheriff's accounts were recorded in the Pipe Rolls: long scrolls that were named for their resemblance to a pipe when tightly rolled. Tally sticks were used to record payments made. The Pipe Rolls extend from 1155 until 1832 and are the longest continual public record in Britain.

The Exchequer system of finance came into existence in Scotland not long after England's was established and worked along very similar lines. Royal finances were vital to keep the country working, especially at a time when war was an ever-present threat, often an aim and always expensive. Richard FitzNigel wrote, 'We are of course aware that kingdoms are governed and laws upheld primarily by prudence, fortitude, moderation and justice, and the other virtues which rules must strive to cultivate. But there are times when money can speed on sound and wise policies, and smooth out difficulties.' The Exchequer was a child of necessity, developed from a cloth to a government department, but its success as an institution is clear.

25. The Common Law Was Born Under Henry II

England, and latterly the United Kingdom, in common with the United States, operates a system of Common Law which sits beside statute law to form the foundation of a legal system of remedies for harm caused. Henry II is viewed as the father of this legal system, delivering equitable justice to all, but it was not the selfless reform it may appear to be.

From the time of King Alfred, who ruled as King of Wessex between 871 and 899, England had been developing a legal system that focused upon the king as the source of justice. With the Norman invasion came a new system of land law and although the Anglo-Saxon legal system was not abandoned it was added to and altered by French influences. The Anarchy of the mid-twelfth century saw a complete breakdown in law and order that allowed chaos to persist and spread unchecked.

Henry II came to the throne at the ending of this period of civil war and held a vast Angevin Empire covering large areas of France and swollen by his lucrative union with Eleanor of Aquitaine. With such a sprawling dominion and in the wake of such immense upheaval Henry needed to find a way to successfully harness his kingdom.

Much of the law in England was based around local custom and the only unified law was that of the Church. Henry spied an opportunity to apply the integrated principles of ecclesiastical law to the application of royal justice. It offered a benefit to the people, who would have a defined law to rely upon irrespective of where they lived, but for Henry it would consolidate his central position as the source and font of all law in his lands.

Judges toured the kingdom applying their new laws in precedence to local custom and the cases that they decided became the body of law themselves. By the thirteenth century three courts operated the Common Law: the Court of Exchequer, the Court of Common Pleas and the Court of King's Bench. Each competed with the others to offer preferential justice to improve their fee income.

During the reign of Henry III (1216-72) a legal tome entitled *On the Laws and Customs of England* was published, probably by the prominent judge Henry de Bracton. It referred to Roman law but was devoted to the English system, under which the law was declared by judicial decisions. Importantly, it also spoke of the need to limit absolute royal power.

Henry II played a vital role in the development of the system of Common Law that remains the basis of the legal system in several nations today, though his motives may owe more to the need to manage unwieldy dominions than a desire for equitable justice for all.

26. Time Immemorial Has a Date

As England's legal system became more codified and people of all social rank became interested in the enforcement of their rights, many cases rested upon the notion of long use, claiming, for example, that sheep had grazed a patch of common land since time immemorial. This concept became a crucial legal matter. How could you prove that something had happened in a time of which there was no memory, living, social or legal?

By the thirteenth century the concept of long custom was causing very real legal issues and the disputes were irresolvable. The Statute of Westminster, issued in 1275, legally codified the date of time immemorial as 6 July 1189. This was the date of the beginning of the reign of Richard I, the Lionheart, and his great-nephew Edward I set that as the point in law at which time immemorial began.

The legal test is therefore whether a right has been held since 6 July 1189. Where a long-established custom exists the courts have stated that there will be a presumption that it was enjoyed since time immemorial unless it can be proven otherwise.

So, curiously, time beyond memory, stretching into the ancient past, actually has a start date.

27. King Arthur, Guinevere and Excalibur Were Discovered by Henry II

Gerald of Wales reports in his chronicle that somewhere between 1191 and 1193 Henry II discovered the tomb of King Arthur, complete with the legendary sword Excalibur. The first problem with this tale is that Henry II died in 1189, so the vague dating of the discovery makes it too late to have been made by Henry. Gerald insists, though, that 'King Henry II of England disclosed to the monks some evidence from his own books of where the body was to be found', so either Henry searched but it was not found during his lifetime, or the information he provided inspired a posthumous search, or the dating of the discovery is a little out.

The grave was discovered at Glastonbury, a place in Arthur's time called the Isle of Avalon. Gerald wrote that in the Old English this means Apple Tree Island, for 'truly that place abounded in apples'. The monks discovered the grave between two stone pyramids, fully sixteen feet into the ground, as many of Henry's sources had suggested it would be. Inside that grave was a large stone cross, upon which was carved, 'Here lies buried the famous King Arthur with Guinevere, his second wife, in the isle of Avalon'. The male skeleton was said to be of enormous proportions and a lock of golden hair identified the other body as a female. There was also a sword within the grave: the sword of King Arthur, the legendary Excalibur.

The monks at Glastonbury kept the bones in an ornate wooden chest and pilgrims flocked to see them. Later, during the reign of Edward I, a black stone sarcophagus was placed next to the High Altar and the bones re-interred. The monastery was dissolved by Henry VIII, the last abbot hung drawn and quartered for treason. There is no record of the fate of the bones.

The stone cross which was found in the grave and identified its occupants was preserved and better documented. That does not mean that it was not a forgery, but it is fairly well recorded by many chronicles over the following centuries. It was last recorded in the possession of William Hughes, Chancellor of Wells, in the early eighteenth century. Then it disappeared.

What of the mighty Excalibur? The story goes that Henry's son Richard I gave the sword as a gift to Tancred of Sicily in 1191 (which again throws doubt upon the dates of the find). It would be an odd fate for the most powerful sword in English history and all that it represented to be given away to a foreign ruler.

The financial rewards bestowed upon the monasteries explain their part in the show. Henry II was under threat from rebellion in Wales and the revelation that King Arthur would not return to save the nation was surely the king's motive for the discovery. The fate of King Arthur remains a mystery.

28. Virtually All Medieval People Knew the World Was Round

There has long been a perception that the backward folk of the medieval age thought that the world was flat and that exploration was limited by the fear of falling off the edge of it. An examination of writings stretching back even before the medieval period quickly and thoroughly dispels this myth.

The Venerable Bede, who lived between 672 and 735, wrote very clearly of the orb of the Earth, insisting,

> We call the earth a globe, not as if the shape of a sphere were expressed in the diversity of plains and mountains, but because, if all things are included in the outline, the earth's circumference will represent the figure of a perfect globe … For truly it is an orb placed in the centre of the universe; in its width it is like a circle, and not circular like a shield but rather like a ball, and it extends from its centre with perfect roundness on all sides.

Medieval writers continued to expound the belief that the world was a sphere, their work supplemented and complemented by the use of Arabic writings and research. Dante's *Divine Comedy* describes the world as a spherical body. Scholars such as St Thomas Aquinas, Albertus Magnus, Roger Bacon, Michael Scot and others wrote of the Earth as a globe throughout the thirteenth century.

Cosmas Indicopleustes, who travelled throughout India from Byzantium in the sixth century, is one of the very few writers to explicitly state that the world was flat, believing that the heavens formed a curved lid over the flat Earth. Cosmas seems to have been in a club of one in his belief and it had no impact on the popular consciousness.

Illuminated manuscripts frequently show the word as a circle and show Christ holding a round earth. The large number of *mappae mundi* that survive from the medieval period, the most famous residing at Hereford Cathedral, invariably represent the earth as round, though, like modern maps and atlases, they are flat. Whilst they cannot represent the world as a globe, they at least confirm the belief that it was circular. The first surviving globe dates from 1492, at the close of the medieval period, but it confirms this was a demonstrably long-held belief.

When Christopher Columbus set sail from the coast of Spain on 3 August 1492 it is often considered a brave move in the face of the risk of falling off the edge of the world. The very fact that Columbus took the route west to try and reach the Indies proves that he knew very well that the world was a sphere. The risk was in being unsure of the size of the sphere and how long it might take to reach the Indies.

29. RICHARD I WAS AN ABSENT KING

Richard I is known to history as Richard the Lionheart and is remembered as a great warrior who excelled on Crusade and cost England a fortune to ransom when he was captured on his return voyage. He died of gangrene that developed from a wound sustained during the siege of Châlus-Chabrol on his way back to England in 1199, but it is likely that neither he nor his subjects mourned the fact that he never made it back.

Richard was born in 1157, the second surviving son of Henry II and Eleanor of Aquitaine. His older brother, Henry the Young King, was destined to inherit the crown and Richard, who was generally considered to have been his mother's favourite, spent many years in her French territories of Aquitaine where she planned for him to rule. Henry II suffered several bouts of rebellion by his children. After the death of Henry the Young King, Richard became heir to the throne but remained at odds with his father.

Having developed a reputation for both chivalry and harshness, Richard became king in 1189. Having already taken the cross in 1187, Richard immediately began preparations to go on Crusade, leaving England in the summer of 1190. In the autumn of 1192, after little success, Richard left the Holy Land. Just before Christmas he was captured on his way home and held to ransom by Leopold, Duke of Austria, who demanded 150,000 marks – over twice the crown's annual income – for the king's release, which was finally secured in February 1194.

Richard spent the next few years trying to reconquer lands in Normandy and was fatally injured as he neared the end of the campaign. During his ten years as king, Richard had spent between six months and a year on English soil. His wife, Berengaria of Navarre, did not set foot in England during their entire eight-year marriage. Richard had overseen the cruel treatment of Jews before his departure and then abandoned his nation to pursue glory in the Holy Land.

Richard's torrid and confused upbringing may have contributed to his lack of interest in his kingdom. England, belonging to his father and his brother, represented conflict, whereas he had spent many years being groomed to rule in his mother's French lands. Perhaps this unhappy association contributed to Richard's willingness to spend nine-tenths of his rule out of the country, in search of the glory that he clearly felt England could not provide.

30. *Droit de Seigneur* is a Post-Medieval Myth

The idea of *droit de seigneur*– 'right of the lord' – or *prima nocta* – 'first night' – feature heavily in medieval fiction as a means to denote the evil lords we should boo and hiss at. The notion has no basis in medieval source material and may have been extrapolated as a later moralistic lesson.

The lord of a manor possessed a great deal of rights over the serfs on his land. One saying goes that a slave owned nothing but his belly. Even the clothes on his back belonged to his lord. Many of these rights focus on marriage, including the prerogative to select a bride for his vassal.

One of the taxes a lord could impose was called *marchet* and was a fee payable to the lord of the manor for his permission for a daughter of his vassal to marry. He could frequently enforce a right to this payment even if she was to be married outside of his manor.

It seems likely that the idea of a lord demanding sexual rights to a bride on her wedding night is a fictitious extension of the idea of *marchet* and became entangled in fiction as a brush with which to tar evil lords with the exercise of immoral rights that they might better be expected to forgo. Certainly no real evidence of this behaviour exists.

31. The Death of Lucy de Vere Shows Medieval Attitudes to Death

Sometime in the early thirteenth century a nun passed away. There were no suspicious or unusual circumstances, but it was an event that clearly demonstrated the medieval preoccupation with death and the fate of the soul.

Lucy de Vere is mentioned as the founder and first prioress of the Benedictine Priory at Castle Hedingham. As Castle Hedingham was the seat of the earls of Oxford, the de Vere family, it seems likely that Prioress Lucy was a relative of the noble de Vere family. The priory was founded in the late twelfth century and at the inspection carried out in 1535 it was home to five nuns and valued at £29 12s 10d per year. It was dissolved in 1536.

The precise date of Lucy de Vere's death is not known. When she passed away the sisters of her priory designed a mortuary roll of over nineteen feet in length. The roll contained images of Lucy's death and of her funeral and when it was completed the nuns sent the mortuary roll around other religious houses in East Anglia requesting their prayers for the departed prioress.

At each stop, the religious houses it visited added their own inscriptions to the mortuary roll commending Lucy's soul for prayer. The mortuary roll is preserved at the British Library and serves as a demonstration of the medieval obsession with death and the passage of the soul through Purgatory and, hopefully, into Heaven.

32. EUSTACE THE MONK INVADED THE CHANNEL ISLANDS

Britain famously counts 1066 as the last time these islands were invaded, at least with eventual success. The truth, even within the confines of the medieval period, is not quite so clear cut.

In 1205 a French mercenary pirate in the employ of King John seized the Channel Islands as a base of operations. Eustace the Monk, also known as the Black Monk, was plying his trade in the Channel when war broke out between England and France. King John hired Eustace to attack French shipping, but was unhappy at his occupation of the Channel Islands and tried to evict him and his men. John declared Eustace an outlaw when he began attacking English shipping too, but found that the pirate's services were worth more than the nuisance of his harassment of English boats. It is possible that Eustace was allowed to build himself a great townhouse in London, such was his worth to the English Crown in disrupting the French.

When England turned on itself during the First Baron's War in 1215, Eustace decided to switch sides and went onto the payroll of the King of France. When the English barons invited Prince Louis, son of the King of France, to invade, Eustace helped to ferry French armies across the Channel and attacked Folkestone.

After King John died in 1216 the war continued. Eustace was transporting reinforcements to Louis in August 1217 when he was intercepted by an English fleet led by Hubert de Burgh. The English sailors used powdered lime to blind Eustace's sailors at the ensuing Battle of Dover and the pirates were defeated. Eustace was found hiding and summarily executed.

The government of the young Henry III, led by William Marshall, was in the process of negotiating peace with France. One of the English demands was the return of the Channel Islands under Eustace's control, but his death put an end to that need.

Eustace the Monk had invaded sovereign English lands in 1205 and occupied them until his death in 1217. Within 150 years of what is considered the last successful invasion of England, a former Benedictine monk from France, operating as a pirate, was in complete control of a portion of English Crown land. It was not the last time such an occupation would take place.

33. MAGNA CARTA DEFINED ENGLISH LAW

King John had ruled for sixteen years by the time he sat down at Runnymede to place his seal upon the Great Charter, surrounded by barons who were actively rebelling against his faltering reign. Within weeks, the Magna Carta lay in tatters and John was at war once again. Magna Carta was later reissued several times and has become one of the most famous documents in medieval history – a cornerstone of Britain's unwritten and the United States explicitly written constitutions, as well as impacting other areas of the Commonwealth. How did such an impotent document achieve such fame?

The Great Charter contained sixty-three clauses in total. One of the vital principles of Magna Carta was that no person was above the rule of law, including the king. Before 1215 the monarch was perceived as the font of all law and justice in the land and, as such, beyond the reach of that which he dispensed. John's exercise of this notion was a core reason that his barons rebelled against him and placing a yoke upon the king to try to keep him under some control was a key aim of the charter.

Three of the clauses contained within Magna Carta remain enforceable today. The confirmation of London and other towns' privileges remains in force, as does the clause protecting the liberties of England's church. Clause 39 states, 'No free man shall be seized or imprisoned, or stripped of his rights or possessions, or outlawed or exiled. Nor will we proceed with force against him except by the lawful judgement of his equals or by the law of the land. To no one will we sell, to no one deny or delay right or justice.'

Throughout John's reign he had arbitrarily imposed taxation to fund unsuccessful military expeditions and imprisoned barons on a whim when he couldn't get his own way. It was to prevent this indiscriminate injustice that the barons forced John to sign the charter and it is no accident that this clause featured.

Weeks after signing Magna Carta, John reneged, obtaining the Pope's approval to do so on the basis that the king had been forced into signing it. The following year the barons invited Prince Louis of France to invade. John fell ill and died trying to defend his crown. His nine-year-old son succeeded as Henry III and an amended version of Magna Carta was reissued to bring the barons back into the fold. The document eventually formed the basis of some of Edward I's landmark legislation.

The provisions of Magna Carta reflected the grievances of the great men of the land. Free men, referred to in Clause 39, made up less than half the population and it did not extend to women either, so its reach was limited. Magna Carta's lasting impact is perhaps more by accident than design, and the deeper significance of Magna Carta is in its legacy, rather than its contemporary implementation.

34. The Charter of the Forest Was More Important than Magna Carta

On 6 November 1217 the young Henry III, under the guidance of his protector William Marshall, sealed and issued the Charter of the Forest. The document was a supplement to Magna Carta to deal with one of the most despised and harmful policies that had grown since the Norman invasion.

William the Conqueror loved hunting, as did his son William Rufus. After the conquest the Norman kings began to reserve some of England's vast forests for their own private use. This brought with it not only expansive private hunting reserves, but also an opportunity for great profit by holding a monopoly on the sale of firewood and the ability to punish those infringing the laws.

Henry II and his sons Richard I and John continued the practice of enclosing royal hunting reserves. This deprived the common man of the ability to forage for food, hunt for meat and gather firewood and was amongst the issues raised at the time of Magna Carta, though significantly it was of less concern to the barons and so failed to be incorporated in the Great Charter itself. Two years later, however, the matter received its own charter, which was reissued alongside Magna Carta in 1225.

The Charter of the Forest effectively reset the lands restricted as royal forests to their state during the reign of Henry II, stating in Clause 3 that 'all woods made forest by king Richard our uncle, or by king John our father, up to the time of our first coronation shall be immediately disafforested unless it be our demesne wood'. Clause 9 restored the right to take wood and graze pigs within royal forests and for pigs to be left in the forest overnight without penalty.

Clause 10 of the charter removed the death penalty as a punishment for poaching venison, confirming that 'no one shall henceforth lose life or limb because of our venison, but if anyone has been arrested and convicted of taking venison he shall be fined heavily if he has the means; and if he has not the means, he shall lie in our prison for a year and a day; and if after a year and a day he can find pledges he may leave prison; but if not, he shall abjure the realm of England'.

It is an important restriction of the charter's reach that it was only to apply to free men in the same way as some provisions of Magna Carta had. This meant that less than half of the population would benefit, but for those free men it was a vital change that reopened access to food and pasture that had been eroded for 150 years. The Charter of the Forest is England's longest standing statute, only being removed from the law books in 1971, and its provisions were probably of far more interest to the common man than those of Magna Carta.

35. MEDIEVAL MONSTERS CONTAIN MORAL WARNINGS

Almost any illuminated manuscript contains odd images of animals engaged in human pursuits. Strange-looking approximations of animals litter the margins: medieval races that no one seemed entirely certain whether or not to believe in. Most disturbing of all, demons are often represented tormenting and torturing people. Each of these images, however playful it may seem, is designed to have a moral angle.

Animals in manuscript art frequently represent the more earthly desires and pursuits of men and women that the monks creating the documents disapproved of. They are often engaged in sport, music or merriment and offer a warning about surrendering to our more animalistic desires.

Monstrous creatures were the stuff of medieval legend, not quite proven fact but evidenced by long-standing stories of what other men had witnessed. One of the legendary species involved the Cynocephalus. Humanoid, but with the heads of dogs, they were believed to live somewhere in the East. There is a story that they even sent a delegation to the pope once. Others included men with their faces in their chests and monopods with one thick leg and a giant foot that they could use to shelter from rain and sun.

These species always existed at the very edge of the known Christian world and offered a warning about what existed where Christianity could not reach. Maps show them in unchartered areas beyond the boundaries of Christianity, urging the need to extend the reach of the Church. Medieval spiritual thinkers became deeply concerned about these races and whether missionaries should seek to redeem their souls, if they possessed such things. If these creatures were descended from Adam and human in nature then it was right to preach the Christian message to them, but if not, it was a waste of time. Often, the wearing of clothes to preserve modesty was used to make the determination.

The representation of demons was a much less subtle but an equally necessary reminder. Demons, the servants of the Devil, were believed to be omnipresent, even if they could not be seen. They tormented people's lives, tempted them to evil and tried to drag their souls to Hell. They were placed throughout manuscripts as a constant reminder of the need for vigilance against an ever-present evil.

The bizarre images that adorn medieval manuscripts and the odd species on the furthest reaches of maps may appear whimsical, but most contain a message, a warning or a challenge, whether it is to control our more primal urges, to seek out those who have yet to hear the Church's message or to be ever vigilant against the servants of evil that await only a lapse on our part to destroy us forever. Whatever the text recounts, the pictures are designed to paint a thousand words.

36. The Medieval Wedding Dress Was Blue

Marriage became a more formalised, legal institution early in the medieval era when a legal requirement for blessing by a priest was created. The bride and groom were required to meet in church and become betrothed around forty days before the wedding took place. The groom would frequently be required to pay a betrothal fee, which was quadrupled as a fine if he then backed out.

The bride would undergo a beauty regime before the wedding as lavish as her family could afford, with her bridesmaids and maid of honour taking care of her. A bride would wear her hair lose as a sign of her purity, as married women were required to tie theirs up and cover their heads. The dress would, if the bride's family could afford it, be blue, the colour of purity. White wedding dresses were popularised by Queen Victoria in the nineteenth century and would not be found at a medieval wedding.

The tiered wedding cake is believed to have its origins in the medieval tradition of guests bringing a small cake or bun as a gift. These were stacked into a pile and the bride and groom would try to kiss over the pile without knocking it over.

In many ways the traditions of a modern wedding would be recognisable to a medieval couple, even the drinking. The term honeymoon is thought to stem from a tradition that the couple were given an unlimited supply of mead for the month following the wedding to aid conception.

The one thing they would certainly find strange would be the dress. White is the (relatively) new blue.

37. THE TOURNAMENT BEGAN AS A WIDE-RANGING MASS BATTLE

Jousting tournaments did not begin as the heavily formulated tilts along the lists by knights in polished armour. Such spectacles only became common at the very end of the period when the tournament became a show rather than practise for the battlefield.

In the twelfth century the tourney grew in popularity throughout Europe. Teams of knights led by a noble lord toured the fields of Europe in search of wealth and glory. Two teams would enact a mock battle lasting for hours and ranging over miles of land. The aim was to knock an opponent from his horse and force him to surrender. The knight taking him into custody could then claim a ransom for his prisoner at the end of the melee.

Successful knights and teams could make their fortune at tournaments. William Marshall was a key member of the tourney team operated by Henry the Young King, son of Henry II, in the late twelfth century. Marshall grew rich and became one of the most famous knights of his age due to his exploits in the tournaments of Europe.

The Tournament of Peace held in Windsor Park in 1278 only allowed the use of whalebone wrapped in parchment and painted silver as swords. In 1292 a Statute of Arms required that no pointed swords, pointed daggers or maces could be used during a tourney. In spite of such provisions, entering a tournament was a dangerous business and could lead to serious injury or death.

The tournament would later become a pageant rather than a practical training exercise. It was war devolved to sport, but its beginnings were very practical.

38. WILLIAM MARSHALL SAVED ENGLAND

One figure dominates the medieval period like no other who was not a king, yet he is a man frequently forgotten. A celebrity of the tourney circuits of Europe and servant to four kings through some of England's most turbulent times, William Marshall saved England from itself and from French conquest.

Born around 1146, William's father had sided with Empress Matilda during the civil war known as the Anarchy. When King Stephen took control this placed William's family on the wrong side of the disputes. In 1152 William was a hostage for his father's good behaviour, but in spite of threats to hang the boy, John Marshall refused to surrender his castle. Stephen refrained from punishing the young William and England would be grateful for decades to come that he had.

After Stephen's death in 1154 William entered the service of Henry II, proving a valiant and loyal knight. In 1170 he was appointed guardian to Henry II's oldest son, Prince Henry. By the time Prince Henry died in 1183 at the age of twenty-eight, William Marshall had overseen the development of the most famous and successful tournament team in Europe under the prince's patronage. In spite of Henry II's sons' frequent rebellions against their father, William remained loyal to the Crown, re-entering Henry II's service and fighting for the king in France in 1187.

When Richard I succeeded to the throne in 1189 William Marshall remained in favour, marrying the daughter of the Earl of Pembroke and acquiring the right to that title on his father-in-law's death. With Richard I abroad on Crusade, William Longchamp,

Bishop of Ely and Lord Chancellor, was left in control of the country, but his relationship with the nobility was strained, a problem added to by Richard's brother John. Marshall joined the nobles to see Longchamp sent into exile, though he also worked to prevent John from seizing power for himself.

On King John's accession in 1199 William helped to see the transfer completed smoothly and now became Earl of Pembroke. A decade later, Marshall was amongst the leading members of John's council, remaining loyal to the king throughout the rebellions that led to Magna Carta. John died during the campaign in 1216 and was succeeded by his nine-year-old son, Henry III. Marshall was appointed the king's protector, supposedly swearing, 'By God's sword, if all abandoned the king, do you know what I would do? I would carry him on my shoulders step by step, from island to island, from country to country, and I would not fail him not even if it meant begging my bread.'

The barons had invited Prince Louis of France to invade and take the crown. London was in French hands when Marshall, now aged about seventy-one, met the invading force at the Battle of Lincoln on 20 May 1217. He won the day and drove the French armies back into the Channel. William concluded a workable peace treaty with Louis and oversaw the reissue of a more moderate version of Magna Carta considered acceptable to the crown. When he died in 1219, William Marshall had served four kings and saved England from foreign invasion.

39. The Dungeon Began Above Ground

The word 'dungeon' began with a very different meaning from that which is associated with it now. This most infamous place of imprisonment was not originally the dark, dank, underground pit that it was to become.

Imprisonment was not a widespread form of punishment during the medieval period. Criminals might be detained prior to sentencing but, if found guilty, punishment would more likely take the form of a fine, time in the stocks or even hanging. Imprisonment was reserved for those who were financially worth keeping. Noble prisoners taken on the battlefield or held for political reasons would come with a hefty ransom that made their imprisonment worthwhile.

Such important, high-value prisoners were always kept in the keep, the most secure part of the castle, high above ground. The original name for a keep was 'donjon' and when lords moved into more comfortable areas of their castles as threats subsided the donjon remained a place to keep anything valuable. Eventually the donjon became accepted into the vernacular as the castle dungeon, though it remained high in a tower so that it was easily secured.

It was late in the medieval period when castles became about show and comfort rather than defence alone, and the area for holding prisoners was moved out of the way, into a part of the castle no one wanted to live in. Only then did the dungeon move underground into the dark, damp parts of the castle.

Things could get a whole lot worse than a dungeon. The *oubliette*, the forgotten room, was a tiny, pitch-black space where prisoners were literally forgotten and from which few emerged alive.

40. THE RELATIONSHIP OF VILLEIN TO LORD WAS ONEROUS

The feudal system is frequently represented as a pyramid, the pinnacle of which represents the monarch, with power flowing down to broader classes. The base of the pyramid, the broadest part taking the greatest weight, was populated by serfs. Even within this level of society there existed a hierarchy with subtle but crucial differences.

The lowest rank of serf was the slave, who was effectively the property of his lord, owned no land and earned no money. This class of serfdom gradually disappeared through the Middle Ages. The second most common type of serf recorded at the time of Domesday was the cotter, who ranked just above a slave. A cotter held just enough land to support a family but was beholden to the lord of the manor.

The most prevalent type of serf was the villein, who ranked above the cotter and could hold a small farm. Like other serfs, the villein was required to pay his lord for the land that he held by working the lord's land. The amount of labour required was contractually defined and tended to vary according to the season. The problem this presented was that as harvest approached the lord would require more work, leaving less time for the villein to work his own land effectively.

A portion of the villein's crop would go to the lord of the manor in tax; he would keep enough to feed his family, but after that he was allowed to sell any surplus at market, offering a chance to accumulate some money. The land held by villeins belonged to the lord but could be passed through a family. The villein was, however, completely tied to the land that he worked.

Top of the class of serfs were the freemen. Relatively uncommon, these men rented their land for a fee and owed little or no service to the lord. Their tenancy was reasonably secure and their money and goods their own.

The weight of the service owed to a lord varied greatly. Some serfs were required to work three days a week on their lord's land, leaving little time to tend their own. Some monasteries were notoriously harsh landlords. Other arrangements were more seasonal. In 1243 the Plea Rolls for Staffordshire record the arrangement between the Abbot of Hales and his tenants, requiring them to plough and harrow for him during Lent, the number of sessions required of them being based on the size of the land they held. It was compulsory to use the abbot's mill but they were free to buy from any market they chose rather than being restricted to his.

In the Middle Ages, as in other times, the lot of the working man depended entirely on the nature of the man he worked for.

41. ROGER BACON PREDICTED THE FUTURE

Living between 1214 and 1292, Roger Bacon resigned his chair at the University of Paris in 1247 to devote the rest of his life to study. Bacon had already delved into the teaching of the ancients and learned from the wisdom arriving in Europe from Arabia. He was perhaps the first scientist in the modern sense of the word and some of his predictions are amazing.

In 1250 Roger set about producing the *Epistola de Secretis Operibus Artis et Naturae*, a work combining his knowledge of art and nature. Bacon not only designed a magnifying glass, but predicted cars, powered ships and manned flight. In his *Epistola* Bacon wrote,

> First, by the figurations of art there be made instruments of navigation without men to row them, as great ships to brooke the sea, only with one man to steer them, and they shall sail far more swiftly than if they were full of men; also chariots that shall move with unspeakable force without any living creature to stir them. Likewise an instrument may be made to fly withall if one sits in the midst of the instrument, and do turn an engine, by which the wings, being artificially composed, may beat the air after the manner of a flying bird.

Made centuries before the invention of the car, plane or steam ship, Bacon was a visionary who acquired the nickname Doctor Mirabilis – the Admirable Doctor during his lifetime and a reputation as a wizard after his death for his interest in Muslim texts.

42. Every Englishman Was Required by Law to Equip Himself with a Bow and Arrows

Military preparedness was always at the forefront of a king's mind during the medieval period. Most of the instruments of government were designed to collect money and measure the number of men available in times of need. In 1181 Henry II issued the Assize of Arms, requiring all knights and freemen to maintain a minimum level of equipment ready for battle. In 1252 Henry III issued an Assize of Arms that changed the course of European history.

The Assize of Arms of 1252 was designed to reinforce the 1181 decree and keep men within the kingdom prepared. There had been peace for some years by this point and that bred complacency. Henry III's Assize, though, made an important new provision too. All men between the ages of fifteen and sixty were legally required to equip themselves with a bow and some arrows. Archery was to become the foundation stone of English military success in the next century.

At the battles of Crécy in 1346 and Poitiers in 1356, the English and Welsh bowmen had proven to be the difference between the English and French armies. In 1363 Edward III bolstered the position of this weapon of mass destruction with a new Archery Law. This required every Englishman to practise with a longbow after church every Sunday without fail. It was declared illegal to indulge in any other sport or pursuit that detracted from longbow training.

The longbow first appeared in Wales in the twelfth century. Standing around six feet tall, it could take up to four years to create a cured-yew bow, but the result was utterly devastating. Longbows had a draw weight of up to 200 pounds and a range of around 400 yards. The arrows they fired could be lethal to a fully armoured knight at 250 yards. A skilled archer was required to loose twelve to fifteen arrows a minute. In a detachment of hundreds, the sky would darken with wave upon wave of deadly shards falling from the air. Arrowhead design was altered depending upon use, with a long bodkin meant to pierce mail armour, a short bodkin to puncture plate and swallowtail heads used to kill horses under their rider.

Many years of training and practise were required simply to draw a longbow to its full weight. Compulsory training made Englishmen of the fourteenth and fifteenth century broad men with dense, solid muscles across their shoulders, backs and arms. The benefit, though, was clear to see. From Crécy to Poitiers and at Agincourt in 1415, the English longbow wrought havoc amongst larger armies, the common men firing their arrow storms felling their noble adversaries and making England a military superpower, remaining unrivalled until the advent of less specialised firearms.

43. Possessed People and Witches Might Have Been High

There are many theories about witchcraft and demonic possession during the medieval era. One possibility lies in the bread that the poor ate when the harvest was bad.

Ergot is a fungal blight that affects rye crops. It tends to appear in a wet spring that follows a cold winter. The characteristics of ergot consumption, known as ergotism, vary from dry, gangrenous skin to convulsions; further symptoms include itching, mania, psychosis, vomiting and diarrhoea.

It has been suggested that cases of witchcraft and demonic possession might have been the effects of ergot infecting the bread supply. The ergot would cause manic, convulsive behaviour and hallucinations which might have been hard to explain as they gripped a person. In the medieval age, anything that could not yet be explained by science could always be explained in terms of religion; God's displeasure, his satisfaction or acts of possession.

It is also possible that ergotism contributed to the spread and devastation of the Black Death. The disease considerably weakens the immune system and may have left many people more prone to the deadly infection of the plague. Some of the symptoms were not dissimilar to the plague and it is possible that cases of ergotism mingled with plague cases to magnify the plague's deadly reputation.

Perhaps medieval cases of witchcraft, demonic possession and even the Black Death were in fact caused by a crop blight that had effects not far removed from LSD. Getting high could lead to real trouble in medieval Britain.

44. Edward I's Cunning Escape Saved the Monarchy

Henry III was not a popular king. In 1265 he was being held in captivity, under the control of Simon de Montfort, 6th Earl of Leicester. Henry's twenty-five year-old son, Prince Edward, was also under de Montfort's power. The earl was the prince's godfather and hoped to negotiate with the young man; Edward appeared to go along with the plan.

In his comfortable imprisonment Edward was visited by friends, including Thomas de Clare, Lord of Thomond, the younger brother of Gilbert de Clare, Earl of Gloucester. Gloucester had originally sided with de Montfort, but the earls had fallen out and Gloucester had changed side. Through these visits de Montfort hoped to reconcile with Gloucester.

On one occasion Thomas de Clare and Edward were allowed to ride out from Hereford, under armed guard, to get some fresh air and to exercise their horses. The young men drove their horses hard, betting which was the fastest. They then took turns to ride the guard's horses in a competition to find the best steed there. After enjoying the sport, the horses were exhausted and unable to run any further – all except one. The two conspirators had kept one horse back and with all of the others unable to run any longer, Edward mounted the fresh steed, reportedly quipping, 'Lordlings, I bid you good day! Greet my father well, and tell him I hope to see him soon, to release him from custody!' With that, he rode from his guards, who were unable to pursue him, and into freedom.

Shortly after Edward's escape he gathered around 10,000 men to give battle to de Montfort. The prince's royalist army boasted twice as many men as de Montfort's force and the two met at the Battle of Evesham on 4 August 1265. Simon de Montfort was killed in the battle and his army was crushed. Edward's father, Henry III, was restored and, although a pocket of resistance held out at Kenilworth Castle for over a year afterwards, the Battle of Evesham marked the end of baronial resistance to Henry III and ushered in a period of peace and unity.

All of this was only made possible by the young Edward's cunning escape and subsequent victory in his father's name. Simon de Montfort had held the reins of power for over a year and had been strengthening the position of Parliament as a check upon the authority of the king. Had Edward failed to escape and win the field at Evesham, England's political landscape may have looked very different for the remainder of the medieval period.

45. SIMON DE MONTFORT REDEFINED PARLIAMENT

On 20 January 1265 a parliament was summoned to sit at Kenilworth Castle. This sitting is considered to have been the first true parliament in England and the man who called it, Simon de Montfort, Earl of Leicester, is remembered as the father of Parliament, at least in a more democratic form. The truth, though, is not quite so clear.

Parliament did not spring into life in 1265. Anglo-Saxon kings operated the Witenagemot, a council of advisors to assist in the operation of government. Papers from the reign of Æthelstan (927-39) demonstrate that up to 100 such men, both secular lords and clergy, attended these gatherings.

Following the Norman Conquest, William I adopted the Witenagemot system, expanding it to include land-owning tenants amongst those whose advice he sought. This increased the notion of a king's accountability to his subjects and by 1215 it was this notion that was being enforced, rather than created, by Magna Carta.

Men of the rank of knight had been attending gatherings at the king's summons for decades. This was also not the first time that attendees had been elected to the post, which had been in occurrence since 1254, more than a decade before de Montfort's 1265 parliament. His parliament is frequently viewed as the first step towards a democratic representative body, but the election of representatives for towns and boroughs was nothing new.

At the Battle of Lewes in 1264, Simon had captured both his brother-in-law Henry III, with whom he had a very up-and-down relationship, and the king's son Prince Edward. His parliament was held in a desperate bid for legitimacy from this position of militarily acquired power and was not at all democratic, being far from evenly representative. Moreover, Simon de Montfort called only twenty-three peers: those known to be supportive of his aims. Peers remaining loyal to the king were excluded. Around 100 members of the clergy were summoned, as they were more sympathetic to de Montfort. Even the local representation was skewed. More supportive towns and areas were asked to send four representatives, whilst less favourable areas were asked for just two.

The word 'parliament' first appears in an official document to describe a gathering of the king's advisors in 1236. Simon de Montfort seems to have passed into legend as the father of Parliament when there was, in fact, nothing new, unusual, revolutionary or controversial about the session that he instigated. He had snatched power in a military coup and sought the support of a body that traditionally approved taxation and legislation. Far from acting as a midwife to democracy, Simon packed his parliament with those he knew would support him. Later in the year he would lose power again. His short-lived regal authority has slipped into legend as a lie.

46. Colchester Abbey Framed the Townsfolk

The relationships between monastic establishments and the communities around them could be a benefit to both, but some did not co-exist in harmony. St John's Abbey in Colchester had a difficult relationship with the town and its people. On one occasion in 1272 matters came to a head, as the monks tried to frame the townspeople for murder.

Two areas of land, Greensted and Donyland, were a constant source of friction between the abbey and the town. In 1255 the town and abbey came to an agreement to divide access to the rabbit warrens there, but in 1270 Henry III had to censure the abbot for infringing the rights of the borough.

At the midsummer fair of 1272 the long-running dispute spilled over into violence and there was a riot, with scrapping between the men of the town and the brothers of the abbey. The morning after the fracas the coroner was summoned by the monks to examine the body of one of their number who had been killed by the townsfolk in the fighting.

The inquest commenced, but an issue arose when there appeared to be no one missing, no one dead who could be identified as the corpse on the green. Finally, the coroner discovered that the dead body belonged to a criminal who had been hanged in the town. The monks had cut the body down and dragged it to the green just so that they could accuse the townsmen of killing one of their order.

Relations did not improve. In the early fifteenth century a gatehouse was erected to protect the abbey from attack by the townsmen. Not all co-existence was happy.

47. The Last Welsh Prince of Wales Died Fighting for Independence

Llywelyn ap Gruffudd was born in the early 1220s, the grandson of Llywelyn the Great and a member of the ancient royal House of Gwynedd. For twenty years in the mid-thirteenth century he maintained a fitful struggle to expand his territories and assert independence from the English crown. The height of his success represented the most united the peoples of Cymru had been in the medieval period and he remains the only Welshman ever to be recognised as Prince of Wales by an English king.

Llywelyn the Great had been succeeded by his oldest legitimate son, Dafydd. Dafydd's brother Gruffudd and one of Gruffudd's sons, Owain, were held as hostages for Dafydd's good behaviour by Henry III, but Gruffudd fell whilst trying to escape through a window in the Tower of London, his death slipping the restraints from Dafydd, who went on the offensive. Henry freed Owain in the hopes of causing an internal dispute, but Owain stayed out of Wales. When Dafydd died in 1246, Owain's younger brother Llywelyn succeeded.

In 1247 Llywelyn signed the Treaty of Woodstock with Henry III, effectively dividing the kingdom of Gwynedd in two, the eastern half being controlled by England and the west by Llywelyn. When Henry tried to further undermine Gwynedd using Llywelyn's brother Dafydd, Owain also betrayed his brother and took the opportunity to vie for power. Llywelyn defeated them at the Battle of Bryn Derwin in 1255, rendering himself sole ruler of Gwynedd. In 1256 the inhabitants of English-controlled East Gwynedd appealed to Llywelyn to liberate them and he happily obliged. In June 1257 Llywelyn won another victory at the Battle of Cadfan.

As Simon de Montfort rose to oppose Henry III in England, Llywelyn swiftly allied himself to him, spying an opportunity to further rid himself of the English king. Simon de Montfort's control lasted only a year, but as Henry III struggled to re-establish himself Llywelyn snatched territory and castles. From this position of strength, Llywelyn negotiated the Treaty of Montgomery in 1267, which granted Llywelyn lordship over all of Wales and the homage of all Welsh lords but one. The price of this was 30,000 marks to be paid in annual instalments, but the treaty would also recognise Llywelyn's title as Prince of Wales. It was too good an opportunity to pass up.

Each year the money proved hard to raise, and Henry III's son, Edward I, proved a much sterner opponent than his father. Llywelyn refused to attend Edward's coronation and in 1276 the English king put a price on his head. In 1277 Edward invaded Llywelyn's lands with ruthless efficiency, cutting off his supply lines. Llywelyn had to surrender and give homage to Edward, but he rebelled again in 1282 and this time Edward fell upon Wales hard, obliterating the royal seat of Gwynedd. Llywelyn, the last Welsh Prince of Wales, was killed on 11 December 1282. Every Prince of Wales since has been the son of an English king.

48. MEDIEVAL MEDICINE WAS BASED UPON THE FOUR HUMOURS

Hippocrates expounded a theory in the fourth century BC that outlasted the medieval era and dominated the understanding of the human body and illness for centuries. The theory was that the human body was made up of and affected by four humours: blood, phlegm, yellow bile and black bile. Wellness lay in the correct balance of these four elements and most illness was thought to be a result of an imbalance – a belief that dictated medical treatments.

Blood was related to the air element and caused a person to be lively and happy. Phlegm equated to elemental water and drew out traits such as patience and tolerance, but made a person introverted. Yellow bile was the fire humour and stoked anger and passion with the body, but also gave great reserves of energy. Black bile represented earth and caused sadness and melancholy, making those with this as their dominant humour moody and prone to depression.

Medieval medical theory taught that diet, a poor environment or disease caused the humours to move out of balance within the body, allowing the prevailing trait of the predominant humour to dictate the mood of the person. Diet was an important feature of correcting the humours, with certain foods capable of cancelling out imbalances. Medicines tended to be herbal remedies that also sought to create balance in the body.

Bloodletting was one of the most common and most famous methods of rebalancing the humours. By drawing imbalanced blood from the body, it was thought that the body was able to rebalance itself and correct the problem. Bloodletting took two main forms: derivation meant bleeding near to the affected area and revulsion meant drawing blood from the farthest part. The use of leeches and cutting became attached to a belief that each vein and artery in the body led back to a specific organ and so bleeding a particular vein worked to correct an imbalance within the organ that it originated from.

Bleeding was regarded as a form of surgery and the tools required could only be used by a licensed barber surgeon, a physician who performed surgery as opposed to the administration of medicines. They treated the wounded on battlefields and often cut hair when war was slow. The red-and-white striped pole that traditionally marks a barber's shop derives from the pattern of blood and bandages that represented their work.

The theory of the four humours lasted for many centuries and was only discredited relatively recently. When a body produced phlegm and bile during illness it seemed to validate the teachings and further drive the pursuit of treatments which would rebalance that which had become imbalanced. There was far more to this than quackery. It was considered solid, scientific practice driven by evidence. Though modern understanding of the human body has caused it to become discredited, the theory of the four humours lasted longer than modern medicine has so far.

49. THE ELEANOR CROSSES MARK THE STOPS OF EDWARD I'S QUEEN'S FUNERAL PROCESSION

Eleanor of Castile was Queen Consort of England from 1272, when she married Edward I, until 28 November 1290, when she died, aged nearly fifty, in Lincoln. Edward I had been devoted to his wife and was left distraught at her passing. He made some of the most lavish funeral arrangements of the medieval era, including monuments to his beloved wife that survive today.

Eleanor's organs, with the exception of her heart, were buried in Lincoln Cathedral. Her heart was transported to the Black Friar's in London. Her body, carefully preserved, was to make a solemn journey to Westminster Abbey to be interred as a queen. The funeral procession took twelve days to reach Westminster and on 17 December she was laid to rest before the High Altar in a spot once occupied by Edward the Confessor. When her own tomb was completed, she was moved to her final resting place.

At each place where the funeral cortège had rested overnight, accompanied for most of the journey by the king himself, Edward ordered the erection of a memorial cross. These tall towers, with images of Eleanor and the royal court of arms adorning each one, were erected between 1291 and 1297 at Lincoln, Grantham, Stamford, Geddington, Northampton, Stony Stratford, Woburn, Dunstable, St Albans, Waltham, Cheapside and Charing.

Three of these crosses, those at Geddington, Northampton and Waltham, have survived to this day as monuments to the power of Edward I and his love for his queen. The Cheapside Cross had been built in the middle of a road, leading to its destruction in 1643. The Charing Cross was pulled down in 1647 to make way for the statue of Charles I on horseback that now occupies the spot, though a replica was placed outside Charing Cross station in 1863.

Queen Eleanor had not been widely liked in England. The Chronicle of Walter of Guisborough, written around fifty years after her death, recalls a contemporary rhyme that jibed 'the king desires to get our gold, the queen, our manors fair to hold'. Edward, though, was clearly besotted. It took him a decade to remarry, and when his second wife gave birth to a daughter he named her Eleanor. The death of Queen Eleanor coincides with a change in Edward I's rule, too. In the decade that followed Edward developed a reputation as a hard, ruthless man, earning the nickname 'the Hammer of the Scots'.

There was also war with France in the years following Eleanor's death. It is possible that the queen had tempered Edward's more hard-nosed, merciless tendencies and that grief and the loss of her calming hand caused him to slip into a decline of ruinous war. It is easy to overlook how much these little human moments can direct history.

50. THE STONE OF DESTINY WAS SEIZED FROM SCOTLAND BY THE ENGLISH

The Stone of Scone, also known as the Stone of Destiny, holds an exalted place in the national consciousness of Scotland. The origins of the block are lost in mystery. Some say that it was a relic from the Holy Land, used by Jacob as a pillow and carried through various flights from danger through Egypt, Spain and Ireland before arriving in Scotland. Other stories tell of the stone being hewn from rock in Ireland or Scotland.

The Stone of Scone is a block of sandstone measuring 660 mm in length, 410 mm in width and 270 mm in depth. Chisel marks can be seen on its surface and it is geologically similar to Scottish sandstone, suggesting that it may not really have travelled from the Holy Land. However, the case may not be so clear cut. In 1296 the stone became a political weapon in the hands of an English king.

Kings of Scotland were traditionally crowned seated on the Stone of Destiny ever since the kings of Dalriada, an area covered today by Argyll, began to use the stone and imbued it with mystical properties. Kenneth I, the thirty-sixth King of Dalriada, moved his capital to Scone in the mid-ninth century when he united the tribes of Scots and Picts into one kingdom. After that, all kings of Scotland underwent their coronation on the stone at Scone Palace for over four hundred years.

John Balliol was the last King of Scotland to be crowned on the Stone of Scone in 1292. As a bitter dispute over the right to the throne broke out, Edward I of England offered to mediate, only to try and snatch the crown for himself. In 1296 he sent men to seize the Stone of Destiny and remove it to London. It was built into the coronation throne at Westminster Abbey and every English and British monarch since Edward II has been crowned sitting above it. Elizabeth II was the last to be enthroned atop the stone before it was returned to Scotland in 1996.

In 1950, a group of students stole the stone and took it to Scotland, only for it to be recovered. There were rumours that they returned a fake, though, and kept the real stone in Scotland. It was not the first time that this tale has been told. There have been rumours ever since 1296 that when the English approached Scone Palace the stone was replaced with a lump of local sandstone, cut to roughly the right size and shape, so that what the English carried away in triumph was a fake. This has been used to explain why a legendary rock from the Holy Land bears a striking resemblance to Scottish sandstone. The real pillow of Jacob never left Scotland.

51. Edward I's Son Was the First English Prince of Wales

England and Wales were frequently at odds. English kings had always claimed lordship over the Welsh princes, who in turn asserted their independence whenever they could. Edward I of England spent much of his time and money trying to suppress the Welsh princes and thoroughly conquer the country. Many of his castles survive in Wales to this day, including Carmarthen, Conwy, Harlech and Aberystwyth.

In 1284 Edward's first son was born. Given his father's name, he also took the traditional identifier of his place of birth, becoming known as Edward of Caernarfon; Caernarfon Castle was one of the fortresses erected by Edward I. 1284 also saw Edward's final victory over the Welsh. The Statute of Rhuddlan effectively annexed Wales to the English crown and it ceased to exist as an independent political entity.

The Statute of Rhuddlan replaced Welsh laws with English ones, dividing the country into English-style counties with Sheriffs appointed to administer justice. One important difference that was imposed was the removal of the right of illegitimate sons to inherit, as had been the tradition under Welsh law.

In 1301, as part of his campaign to ensure Welsh absorption, Edward I created his son Prince of Wales, a title traditionally claimed by the most prominent amongst the rulers of the Welsh regions. The seventeen-year-old prince was also created Earl of Chester and granted lands throughout North Wales. The move was designed to assert the English crown's control over Wales and also to create an independent power base for the king's oldest son. Ruling Wales would serve to prepare him for one day becoming king.

After succeeding to the throne in 1307, Edward II did not create his own oldest son, later Edward III, as Prince of Wales. Edward III would reinstate the tradition, creating his own oldest son Prince of Wales. From that point onward every monarch to have a son has created their heir Prince of Wales. Originally intended as a tool of control, the position became a form of apprenticeship for kings-to-be that has lasted to the present day.

52. Medieval Armour Was Designed for Manoeuvrability

Armour was not the reserve of the rich and powerful. Few men would take to the field without some form of protection. Even at the height of the use of plate armour in the early fifteenth century a knight's mobility was a crucial part of the design of his protection. If he was stuck in one place and one position he would not last long on a battlefield, no matter how thick the steel surrounding him might be.

A typical suit of armour would have weighed around 50 lbs – about 22 kg. This is less than a modern British army infantryman, whose kit weighs an astonishing 145 lbs, with basic survival kit accounting for 57 lbs of that weight. Each element of a suit of armour was carefully designed and skilfully constructed by an armourer to allow as much freedom of movement as possible.

The notion that knights had to be hoisted into their saddles has no contemporary basis. Sir Laurence Olivier showed this practise in his film *Henry V*, but he did so in spite of advice from the Master of Armouries at the Tower of London at the time that the need for and practise of this had no basis in fact.

Knights had to be able to get back to their feet swiftly and on their own if they were knocked down in the heat of battle. Lying prostrate in the press of a crowded battlefield would mean certain death, either by blade or by being crushed underfoot. There have been many experiments in movement wearing late medieval armour or faithful reconstructions and all show that movement is remarkably free and unrestricted even in full plate armour. A superb and fascinating example of mobility in full late medieval plate armour can be found in Musée de Clumy's YouTube channel entitled 'Le combat en armure, Daniel Jaquet'.

The mobility of British knights was improved by the use of leather straps to secure the pieces rather than having riveted metal fixings. The downside of this design is that, because leather straps would rot and might snap in battle, pieces of armour could be lost. They might have been reused by those who found them or remain lost in the mud. There are no surviving medieval suits of English armour in existence today, but this more disposable approach meant that when it became less common it was not as well preserved as some continental examples.

Some later forms of tournament armour might be more rigid and heavier, but they were not designed to be worn for prolonged periods, nor for ease of movement. Functional armour was carefully designed to facilitate ease of movement in combat situations for its wearer. Cumbersome, limiting armour would have been useless and even dangerous to the wearer and it is a testament to the skill of the medieval armourer that protection and movement were so carefully balanced.

53. William Wallace Died for Scottish Independence

In May 1297 a man appeared, as if from nowhere, in Lanark in central Scotland and began a war. Next to nothing is known of William Wallace's early years, but in his mid-twenties he set a nation alight with the hope of freedom. The story of a man who became known as Braveheart has been given the Hollywood treatment so well that the truth has been obscured by the myth.

Wallace's date of birth ranges widely, though the most commonly suggested year is 1272. His parentage is a matter of debate too. He is traditionally recorded as the son of Sir Malcolm Wallace of Elderslie, near Paisley, a minor noble. Wallace's own seal, applied to the Lubeck Letter in 1297, names him as 'William, son of Alan Wallace' and an Alan Wallace was recorded as a contemporary Crown tenant of land in Ayrshire.

So little is known for certain of Wallace's origins that it is no wonder myths were created to fill the gaps. It is not known whether Wallace was married or had any children, nor precisely what sparked his seismic rebellion. There has also been conjecture that he was a thief on the run from the English authorities when he began his campaign.

In May 1297 Wallace and a small band of men attacked the English authorities in Lanark and killed the sheriff. Scotland had been undergoing a succession crisis since the previous year and Edward I of England had offered to help settle the matter, only to impose himself upon Scotland, making the most of the chaos that was keeping the country unsettled. The English quickly became an occupying force, hated by the Scots, and when Wallace struck this first blow men swarmed to his cause and a very real rebellion on a national scale began.

September 1297 saw Wallace's most famous victory at the Battle of Stirling Bridge. By now his force had joined with that of Andrew Moray, the son of a knight who had been leading resistance to the English in the north of Scotland throughout the summer. Wallace and Moray lay in wait at Stirling Bridge, a crossing over the River Forth that the English were to use. Only able to cross two abreast, the Scots waited until a suitable number of English had made the crossing and then attacked, slaughtering them and sending the rest of the English army fleeing in panic.

Wallace was knighted and named Guardian of the Kingdom, but a reversal soon followed in July 1298 when Wallace lost the Battle of Falkirk to a refocused English army. Resigning the guardianship, which passed to Robert Bruce and John Comyn, Wallace made diplomatic efforts abroad, especially in France. On his return in 1305 he was betrayed for the huge bounty placed on his head. Hauled to London and convicted at a show trial at Westminster Hall, Wallace was hung, drawn and quartered on 23 August 1305. However, over 700 years later his cause remains strong.

54. LINCOLN CATHEDRAL WAS THE TALLEST BUILDING IN MEDIEVAL EUROPE

Lincoln Cathedral is notable for many reasons. Building commenced in 1088 when a large Norman castle-like church was birthed. In the early twelfth century a fire ravaged the cathedral and in 1185 an earthquake caused more damage that had to be repaired. At this point Hugh, Bishop of Lincoln, began a large rebuilding program. Hugh was canonised in 1220 and work began on building a shrine to him, but was curtailed when the central tower collapsed in the 1230s.

The cathedral is the third largest in Britain in terms of floor space, only outdone by St Paul's in London and York Minster. In the early fourteenth century the Cathedral's tower was topped with a leaded steeple that made Lincoln Cathedral the tallest building in medieval Europe. For over 200 years Lincoln boasted the title, which was only lost in 1548 when the spire blew down.

55. Edward II's Death Remains a Mystery

It is one of the best-known stories from English history. On 21 September 1327 the deposed Edward II was murdered at Berkeley Castle by having a red-hot poker inserted in his rectum to destroy his internal organs. The method was chosen in order to leave no external marks on the body to betray the murder. A horn was even pushed in first to prevent external burning. A funeral cortege took the wrapped body from Berkeley Castle to Gloucester Cathedral where the tomb can be found today.

That is not quite the end of the story, though. Three years later, in 1330, Edward II's brother Edmund, Earl of Kent, was executed by Roger Mortimer, the de facto ruler during the minority of Edward's son Edward III. Edmund was arrested for trying to free his brother, which is evidence that he at least suspected that his brother was still alive.

Suspicion about the true fate of Edward II has been fuelled by tantalising glimpses that have been unearthed. Edward III's financial accounts for the years 1338/9 make reference to William the Welshman, who was brought before Edward III at Cologne claiming to be the king's father. The man was entertained by the king and was not punished in any way for his claims. Edward II had been born at Caernarfon in Wales and was created the first English Prince of Wales, so the use of the name might have been a reference to his origins.

An undated letter was revealed in 1877 which appeared to be sent by Manuele de Fieschi, a papal notary, to Edward III recounting the escape of the king's father from Berkeley Castle and his journey to

Lombardy in Northern Italy via Ireland, France and Germany. Some historians suggest that Edward II lived out his days in Italy and that his son was not only aware of the fact but corresponded with his father and perhaps even visited him there.

One chronicler wrote at the time of Edward II's supposed death that the wrapped body was displayed only 'superficially', giving lie to the poker story having been designed to leave no mark for display. The swift wrapping and funeral meant that any corpse could have been placed in the vault within Gloucester Cathedral. Edward II had proved ill-suited to kingship and perhaps decided to see out his days in peace, happy for his capable son to rule instead.

The story of the poker was not contemporary and may have been an added embellishment used as a moral tale, a reference to Edward II's suspected homosexuality. The gruesome death was an ethical message designed to give another dimension to the story of Edward II's failures. If he died in 1327 it was almost certainly not caused by a red-hot poker. It is possible that he didn't die then at all. The truth will, for now at least, remain a mystery.

56. People Knew How to Find Safe Drinking Water in Medieval Europe

It is an accepted idiom that medieval people drank beer for breakfast, as well as the rest of the time, because water was too dirty and disease-ridden for human consumption. As far as this idea has worked its way into the consciousness of the modern idea of the past, it is simply not true.

Medieval literature is littered with references to drinking water. It seems to be widely accepted that most would drink watered wine and that is certainly true. The addition of water to wine suggests an acceptance that the water was safe to drink. It is also true that the fermentation process purifies water, rendering unsafe drinking water consumable. Although people in the middle ages did not fully understand the reason that this might be the case, it was noted as a side effect of the brewing process.

As early as 1237 Henry III requested that the springs and waters of Tyburn be granted to the citizens of London, because the city's water supply from its wells was no longer sufficient. A system of wooden and lead piping moved the water from Tyburn along the Strand and Fleet Street, through Ludgate and into the Great Conduit in Cheapside. This became the first public water supply in London.

The course of the conduit attracted vintners and brewers who needed the water – in the fourteenth century Elias de Conductu kept the Tavern of the Conduit. It was clearly understood, though, that the water was meant for the rich to use in the preparation of food and for the poor to drink. Several other conduits were created over the following centuries.

The Little Conduit ran off the Great Conduit and one was created at Cripplegate by the executors of William Eastfield's will. Payments from benefactors for the repair and upkeep of the conduits were frequent, demonstrating their importance to the city.

Doctors did seem to consider it preferable to drink beer and wine wherever possible, believing that there was more nutrition to be had in those drinks and that an excess of water would lead to weakness and debilitation, but not that it was poisonous. It was widely understood that water that had a bad odour should not be drunk. As early as the mid-twelfth century St Hildegard of Bingen wrote that 'it is more healthful and sane for a thirsty person to drink water, rather than wine, to quench his thirst'.

Contrary to what remains a popular conviction, water was widely drunk throughout the medieval period. It was understood that not all water was safe to drink, but also that the establishment of a clean and plentiful supply of drinking water was vital and eminently achievable. No beer for breakfast, unless, of course, that was a personal preference.

57. Edward III Seized Control and Defined His Kingship

Edward III had been king for three years, but at nearly eighteen years of age he had virtually no power. In 1330 he took control of his own destiny and set the tone for his kingship. By the time he died in 1377 he had transformed England into the military power house of Europe. The date that the nation's journey began was 19 October 1330.

Edward III's father, Edward II, had been forced to abdicate in favour of his son following bitter disputes between the nobility. Edward's mother, Isabella of France, had been engaged in a well-publicised affair with Roger Mortimer and the two had forced Edward II to give up his throne to his fourteen-year-old son in 1327.

As the new king was a minor, Mortimer had imposed himself as regent with Isabella's support. He set about gathering great wealth and power to himself, creating himself Earl of March. He was never going to be keen to give up power as Edward came nearer to the age of majority. In March Mortimer had tried and executed Edward's uncle Edmund, Earl of Kent. It was perhaps this that alerted Edward to the need for action.

A few weeks before Edward's eighteenth birthday he was at Nottingham Castle, where Parliament had been in session for three days. Mortimer was rumbling around the castle like a thunderstorm, furious that the Earl of Lancaster had been given rooms near to Isabella when he was not to be trusted. Mortimer gave orders that the guards were to follow his instructions above those of the king.

Edward decided that he had to act, but he was closely

watched and denied any real power. His friends were hauled one by one before Mortimer for interrogation as his suspicions of a plot grew. A plan finally formed when William Eland, a steward in the castle, confided in Edward that there was a secret passage that led up to the chambers occupied by Mortimer and Isabella. Edward sent Eland to a close friend, William Montagu, who had been questioned by Mortimer, and made plans to feign illness to excuse himself that evening. Montagu swung into action with a small band of Edward's friends and the young knights were led through the dark passages and up the secret staircase by Eland.

In the middle of the night the armed men burst into the queen's apartments, which were only lightly guarded. They slew any who stood in their way and seized Mortimer and his two sons. On 29 November Mortimer was hanged at Tyburn. Edward was king now, in reality as well as in name. The brave actions of a small group of devoted, loyal friends had won Edward his freedom and authority and this pattern was to define Edward's kingship. He inspired his men, bound them to him and rewarded them richly, earning himself the title of the Perfect King and propelling England onto the world stage.

58. Livery and Maintenance Meant More than Clothing and Feeding a Household

In many ways the narrative of the politics of the medieval period is the decline of the system of livery and maintenance. Birthed at the outset of the era, its demise coincided with sweeping changes across Europe that marked the closure of the medieval time.

The feudal system was based upon a pyramidal cascading of responsibilities and allegiances. A king would keep the loyalty of his most powerful nobles by offering them good lordship, justice and prosperity. In return he would expect their loyalty and their military support whenever and wherever it was needed. Lords maintained a broader network of minor nobles and knights who they would take care of and who in turn would provide that military muscle when called upon.

Livery was the provision of clothing to those within a lord's care. This might range from ceremonial robes for noble wards within his household, to basic clothing for servants; all would wear the badge of their lord, demonstrating the breadth of his power and, in the quality of the clothing provided, his wealth.

Maintenance did not refer to providing food for the upkeep of a household or retainers, but rather to the maintaining of the causes of those comprising the lord's affinity. A noble would maintain his affinity by offering them a form of recourse to resolve their grievances. He would support those loyal to him in legal matters or to get what they wanted if they felt that they could not achieve their ends through more official channels. The system of maintenance, however, was open to corruption. A lord might choose to support unscrupulous and unjust causes and sometimes the weight and influence he held ensured justice was not done.

By the fourteenth century great lords had developed affinities that influenced their peacetime duties alongside their traditional military service, holding public offices arranged for them by their lord so that his man was in place should he be needed. Richard II began the process of legislating to control affinities, but with little success. In the fifteenth century noble houses such as the Neville, Percy and Beaufort families were able to contribute to delivering the country into civil war because of the huge affinities at their disposal and the sheer number of men they were able to put into the field.

The over-mighty noble reached a pinnacle with Richard Neville, Earl of Warwick. He is remembered by history as the Kingmaker because his power made him able to make and break kings almost at will. The medieval chivalric ideal of service to a lord had become so corrupted that it brought about the disintegration of an era when it toppled.

59. THE LITURGY OF THE HOURS DEFINED MONASTIC LIFE

Prayer dominated medieval life. The Church taught that men should pray all of the time, but within monastic communities the day was broken down by a set schedule of worship known as the Liturgy of the Hours. This broke every day into eight distinct sessions of prayer and song.

The Liturgy of Hours in use throughout the medieval period was largely defined by Saint Benedict of Nursia in the sixth century. The Benedictines are most closely associated with St Benedict, but most monastic orders were based around his *Rule of St Benedict*.

Matins was the first session of the day, celebrated at sunrise. During the first hour of sunlight came Prime, followed at the third hour after sunrise by Terce. Sext was celebrated at the sixth hour of daylight and None at the ninth hour.

Vespers was attended at the end of the day and Compline signalled bedtime throughout the monastery. During the night the monks would attend Vigils and at sunrise it would begin again with Matins.

This cycle ordered the day of every monk within a monastery and all of their other work, agriculture, trade and preaching, had to fit around the requirement of worship that defined their existence.

60. St George Was Adopted as England's Patron Saint for His Chivalry and to Annoy the French

On 19 July 1333 the twenty-year-old Edward III rode into the Battle of Halidon Hill against a Scottish army in pursuit of their country's independence. Above the young king's head fluttered the banner of St George. It was the beginning of a relationship that would see the saint's reputation launched into legend.

St George was not English. He died in Palestine at the turn of the fourth century – a martyr, so the legend goes, because when the Emperor Diocletian ordered that all the Christians within his army be arrested and that all others make a sacrifice to the Roman Gods to prove their true faith, George presented himself to the emperor and declared himself a Christian. A son of one of Diocletian's advisors and a skilled military leader, the emperor did not want to lose George, but no amount of gold or land would sway him. He was tortured and eventually beheaded for his faith.

George eventually became the patron saint of Portugal, Georgia, Lithuania and Venice, as well as England. Much of his story is legend – Pope Gelasius counting George amongst the saints 'whose names are justly reverenced among men, but whose actions are known only to God' – and his slaying of a dragon to save a princess is entirely apocryphal. The attraction of St George to the military mind is clear. Unlike patron saints who championed the conversion of heathens to Christianity, George represents courageous martyrdom: the willingness to fight oppression and injustice and to die if necessary for a just cause. What could be a more fitting model for a knight?

It is this connection that truly led to St George's adoption as the patron saint of England at the outset of the Hundred Years War. St George had long been the patron saint of all knights: a representative of chivalry and a knight's commitment to the pursuit of justice. The birthplace of chivalry and knighthood was France, and they were proud of it. In 1346, when Edward marched an English army to fight a much larger French force at Crécy, he did so under the banner of St George. And he won. Edward had invested heavily in military technology, spearheading the use of the cannon, crossbow and longbow. He shot the French knights in their saddles before they could even begin their charge. This mode of warfare was so alien to the chivalric rules of the French and so devastatingly effective that it established England as the dominant military power in Europe for decades. St George had abandoned the French knights in favour of the English.

Edward III became responsible for the birth of an English national identity, as he unpicked the ties that had long bound England to the Continent. He also adopted English as the official national language. Perhaps his most enduring gift to that new nation, however, was a saint who represented steadfast courage and determination in the face of threat and injustice.

61. Medieval Proverbs Stand the Test of Time

Many of the things we say are so much a part of our everyday life that we rarely stop to think why we say them. Some of these sayings and proverbs can be traced back a thousand years and would have been uttered by the lips of medieval folk every bit as casually as they are today.

Egbert of Liege compiled a poem entitled *The Well-Laden Ship*. It was a Latin work designed for beginner students trying to get to grips with the language. It contains early versions of nursery rhymes, such as Jack Sprat, and folk tales, including the earliest known version of Little Red Riding Hood. Egbert put his work together in the eleventh century, as the medieval period was beginning, and he added several proverbs that must have been familiar then and some that remain in use today.

The Well-Laden Ship includes Latin reproductions of 'Don't look a gift horse in the mouth' – literally translated as, 'When a horse is offered for free, you should not open its mouth.' – 'While the cat's away, the mice shall play' and 'The apple never falls far from the tree', all of which are well-recognised ten centuries after Egbert wrote them down. John Warkworth, a London merchant who wrote a chronicle in the mid-fifteenth century, repeated a proverb in one part that runs, 'Such goods as were gathered with sin, were lost with sorrow.'

Other proverbs included in the poem have not stood the test of time so well, but were probably well known in the medieval period. 'A poor man extends his poverty when he has regular recourse to wine' seems to remain good sense. 'The crow, by not crowing, could have the corpse to himself' offers wisdom for those who draw attention to what they have. 'Calves should not play with an ox as they are outmatched in horns' is a clear warning. 'A living dog is better than a dead lion' seems a parallel notion to 'a bird in the hand is worth two in the bush', which appears later in medieval literature.

Other Latin proverbs appear throughout the medieval era: 'He who serves two masters, serves neither'; 'God meets every man, but few recognise Him'; 'In God's sight, nothing ever remains un-avenged'; 'Nature surpasses art without effort or anxiety'.

Some medieval proverbs were less than politically correct. 'No mother-in-law is pleasing to her daughter-in-law unless she is dead' is hardly friendly, even if it raises some knowing smiles. 'A good woman is rare. If, by chance, you find one, she fell from Heaven' is hardly very charitable. Warkworth also used a proverb when recording the siege of St Michael's Mount: 'A castle that will speak and a woman that will hear, they shall be won both.'

One truth recorded in *The Well-Laden Ship* certainly stands any test of time: 'Shit smells more foul the more it is stirred by turning over.'

62. The First Dukedom in England Was Created by Edward III

Edward III was obsessed with Arthurian legend and chivalric deeds. In 1337 he created an entirely new rank and title within his kingdom for his firstborn son and heir. The seven-year-old Prince Edward became Duke of Cornwall, a title still associated with the heir to the monarch. Over the rest of the medieval period sixteen ducal titles were created at various times, causing the most controversy when they strayed outside of the royal family.

In 1337 no one was entirely sure what this new rank really meant. It seemed reasonably clear that a duke was intended to stand above the ancient rank of earl, but just how far above an earl and how far below the king was a matter yet to be proven. The next dukedom was created in 1351 for one of Edward III's closest friends and most loyal supporters, Henry of Grosmont, as a reward for his service. Created Duke of Lancaster, a promotion of the family's earldom, Henry was a great-grandson of Henry III.

When Henry died in 1361 his title passed to his son-in-law, John of Gaunt, third son of Edward III. Unable to leave his second son out, Edward created Lionel Duke of Clarence on the same day that he allowed John to become Duke of Lancaster. Edward III would create no further dukedoms, though his grandson Richard became Duke of Cornwall on his father's death.

The next dukes appeared in 1385, when Richard II elevated his other two uncles. Edmund became Duke of York and Thomas was made Duke of Gloucester. A symptom of Richard II's growing unpopularity emerged in 1386 when he created his favourite, Robert de Vere, 9th Earl of Oxford, as Duke of Ireland. Robert was the first non-royal to be created a duke and it caused outrage, even though it was designed for his lifetime only. The title was forfeited just two years later.

Richard II's cousin Henry Bolingbroke was made Duke of Hereford in 1397, shortly before the two fell out. On the same day the king made his cousin Edward, son of the Duke of York, Duke of Aumale, his half-brother John Holland Duke of Exeter and his half-nephew Thomas Holland Duke of Surrey. Thomas Mowbray was created Duke of Norfolk at the same time.

The next new dukedom was that of Bedford, created for John, the second son of Henry IV, in 1414. Somerset and Suffolk were made for the Beaufort and de la Pole families respectively in 1448, marking Henry VI's favourites. In 1483 the dukedom of Norfolk was recreated for the Howard family.

When the title of duke arrived in England in 1337 no one really knew what it would mean. It came to signify an elite rank in society, usually reserved for close members of the royal family, but occasionally embracing men the king wished to mark as special to him. It was sometimes a poisoned chalice.

63. THE PRINCE OF WALES EARNED HIS SPURS AND STOLE HIS FEATHERS

The Battle of Crécy on 26 August 1346 was the first major engagement of the Hundred Years War, as Edward III sought to enforce his claim to the throne of France. The English army faced a French army of around three times their number on French soil, but the French were to be undone by a devastating new military tactic.

Edward III used his longbowmen and cannon to devastating effect. The French knights were simply unable to comprehend the carnage caused in a fashion so lacking in chivalry, by men other than knights. The French casualties ran to over 2,000, whilst the English lost only a few hundred. The victory set a tone for decades of warfare.

The oldest son and heir of Edward III, the sixteen-year-old Edward, later known as the Black Prince (for reasons that are unclear, but reputedly related to black armour that he wore rather than a dark reputation), was getting his first taste of battle. A messenger arrived at Edward III's position to request assistance for the Prince of Wales, who was in the thick of the fighting. The king asked whether his son was dead or wounded. When the messenger confirmed that he was neither, but fighting strongly, Edward III famously replied, 'I am confident he will repel the enemy without my help,' before turning to one of his companions and remarking, 'Let the boy earn his spurs.'

Another notable combatant, who took the field with the French army, was John, King of Bohemia. John was the oldest son of Henry VII, Holy Roman Emperor, and was also King of Poland and Count of

Luxembourg. John was fifty when he entered the fray at Crécy, but that was not what made his presence remarkable; King John of Bohemia had been blind for a decade before Crécy. When he heard that his own son was caught up in the main action John instructed his men to lead him forward. Tying their bridles together, his guard led their king into the fighting. John said that he wanted to land just one blow with his sword, though Froissart records that he struck four before he was killed, his body was found the next morning along with those of his men, their horses still tied together.

After the battle, the Black Prince appears to have been moved by John's bravery in spite of his obstacles. Prince Edward took the King of Bohemia's insignia and the motto that he used for his own. The insignia was three ostrich feathers and the motto was 'Ich Dien' – 'I Serve'. The emblem and motto remain those used by the Prince of Wales to the present day. It had been the intention of Edward III that his young son should earn his spurs on that day, but instead he earned his feathers and created a piece of history.

64. Medieval Football Was a Large-Scale Brawl

Two teams of eleven engaging in a highly structured and formalised ninety minutes of professional sport is not what anyone in the medieval period would recognise as football. What might now be termed football hooliganism is probably closer to the medieval notion of the game.

The origins of a game resembling football are obscure. It is possible that it travelled from France with the Norman Conquest and involved a solid ball of leather or even wood. It was only later that someone discovered that an inflated pig's bladder bounced, probably unevenly due to the shape, and that this added to the fun. The tendency of the bladder to burst may be what led to it being encased in leather to protect it.

The actual game involved the designation of a target – a goal – to which the ball must be carried. It might be a landmark in the village, a wall or a boundary. Villages might play against each other by designating a spot in each other's village to try and get the ball to. Quite how the ball arrived there was not defined in the rules. Hundreds of men might take part in what was basically a brawl masquerading as a sport.

The ball could be kicked, thrown or carried. Players could be pushed, punched or kicked. As long as the ball reached its goal, anything could happen. The growing popularity of this pastime may have been behind the provision in Edward III's 1365 Archery Law that any sport interfering with statutory bow practise was to be illegal. Early in the following century James I of Scotland issued a statute stating, 'The King forbids that no man play at fute-ball under the pain of fifty schillings to be raised to the Lord of the land, as oft as he be tainted, or to the Sheriff of the land or his ministers, if the Lords will not punish such trespassers.' The last provisions seem to suggest that the nobility were unlikely to enforce the criminalising of football.

Other sports existed throughout the medieval era. Quoits involved throwing a ring of stone over a post. The player with the most rings on the post would win. London Bridge involved two players making an arch as other walked underneath. At the end of a verse of 'London Bridge is Falling Down' the arch was lowered and the trapped player was out. Hopscotch courses could run to 100 feet in length. Bear-baiting was a popular blood sport guaranteed to draw crowds of spectators.

Perhaps the oddest popular game was Hot Cockles, which involved one player bending over with their face in another player's lap, while one of the other players spanked them. The aim of the game was to correctly identify who was spanking you. Is it any wonder that something a little more lively and inclusive was so favoured?

65. Edward III Fought Under Lord Manny's Banner in Secret

Sir Walter Manny, 1st Baron Manny, is one of those enigmatic characters largely forgotten to history, but whose story almost beggars belief. Walter was the fourth son of a French nobleman from Masny in Northern France, born around 1310. In late 1327 he travelled to England in the entourage of Philippa of Hainault as she made the journey to marry the young King of England, Edward III. It was a move that would define his fortunes.

Manny was involved in Edward III's early campaigns in Scotland and must have acquitted himself well, because when Edward decided to invade France he took Manny along with him. It was here that Manny would develop an almost comedic reputation for daring that bordered on wilful carelessness.

In 1342 the town of Hennebont was under siege by the French army after its lord had been arrested and its lady refused to surrender. According to legend, Lady de Montfort was in a council meeting and on the verge of giving up the battered town when she absently gazed out of a tower window, only to see a fleet of ships flying the cross of St George sailing up the river. At its head was Walter Manny, who, ignoring a truce made with the French, had come to provide aid to a potential ally. At one point in the siege Manny led a lightning strike against one of the French siege engines because it was disturbing his lunch.

A few years later Manny was also instrumental in the defence of Aiguillon when it came under siege by a vast army led by the son of the King of France. Manny ventured out on a daily basis to harry the French and gather supplies. When his small force was attacked while foraging by a group said to be six times their number, Manny's horse was killed from under him and all of his men slaughtered. When another party arrived to try and save them they found Manny, standing alone, surrounded by Frenchman and fighting like a cornered lion.

The French attempt to snatch back Calais in 1349 saw Manny, now a lord, on fine form once more. Edward III was in the town, unbeknownst to anyone. Word of the French plan reached him – a small force was to bribe their way into the town, open the gates and signal the army to attack – and a trap was laid. When the French advance party was led into a small tower room they were confronted by an armoured Manny, who rushed at them, sword raised, shouting the famous battle cry of 'Manny! Manny to the rescue!' He halted suddenly and lambasted the men for thinking they could take Calais with so few. The shocked Frenchmen surrendered and the signal was given. The trap snapped shut on the advancing French, with Manny bellowing his war cry as Edward III fought beside him under Manny's banner. An odd hero, indeed.

66. The Black Death Was a Bubonic Plague, but Might Not Have Been Carried by Rats

During 1347 a terrible plague appeared in Europe. By the following year it had crossed the Channel and taken hold in England. The Black Death would decimate populations wherever it reached, but the nature of the disease and the method of its movement remain subjects of debate.

The plague spread unchecked throughout Britain. Estimates of casualties vary widely, but it is likely that around 60 per cent of Europe's population was killed during the epidemics. In Britain, some villages were completely wiped out by the disease. Reported symptoms included fever, headaches, weakness and large swellings at the lymph nodes, primarily in the victim's armpits and groin. Symptoms became apparent within a week of infection and death was painful.

In 2013 twenty-five skeletons were excavated from Charterhouse Square during work on the London Underground. The remains are believed to have belonged to victims of the Black Death during the mid-fourteenth century. DNA of the virus that had killed them was extracted from their teeth and compared to recent outbreaks of the disease. The centuries-old DNA was found to be almost identical to the disease as it exists today.

There is still some discussion over the impact of pneumonic plague during the epidemic. This variant of the disease causes the symptoms of pneumonia, including fever, vomiting and coughing, but lacks the swelling of the lymph nodes. The pneumonic plague is an airborne disease that will take hold more easily in ill and malnourished bodies. Some researchers believe that the pneumonic element of the plague is the only way to explain such a rapid spread throughout Britain. It is possible that the bubonic and pneumonic versions of the plague combined to exacerbate the problems, as the poorly nourished population, unable to fight the infection, succumbed in frightening numbers.

The black rat is seen as the traditional carrier of the disease as it spread. The fleas carried by the rats bit humans, infecting them with the illness and allowing it to move great distances at incredible speed. Research in Oslo is challenging this accepted view by suggesting that the carriers were, in fact, giant gerbils from Asia, where the climate suited the incubation of the disease and the growth of both the gerbils and their fleas. With trade between Asia and Europe at a peak during this period, it is suggested that the Silk Road may have been the Black Death's route into Europe. It is possible that the black rat then became a second carrier.

The method of its lightning-fast spread and the precise nature of the disease, or diseases if more than one variant was at work, remain the subjects of speculation and research. It is certain that to a medieval society there was only one explanation for such apocalyptic death with no hope of salvation: The plague was a punishment from God. In the medieval mind, the unexplained could always be attributed to sin.

67. England's National Identity Was a By-Product of War

From the Norman Conquest onwards French had become the language of the elite in England. Latin was the international language of the Church throughout Europe, but with the arrival of a Norman king and his lords Old English was supplanted in the circles of power. This did not, however, wipe out the indigenous language. French was the language of power and there were plenty without power who retained their Anglo-Saxon language.

England effectively became an outpost of the duchy of Normandy and later, when the Angevin Empire of Henry II brought more continental property to the king's portfolio, the ties with vast swathes of France were drawn tighter still. French was the language of Parliament and of the law, keeping both beyond the reach of the common people. Ironically, this bond only began to fray when England actually laid claim to the French crown.

When Philip VI of France snatched Edward III's duchy of Aquitaine following the English king's refusal to do homage for his French territories, Edward reacted by claiming Philip's crown. Edward was a grandson of king Philip IV of France through his mother, Isabella. Three of Edward's uncles had been kings of France in succession and none had left a male heir. As French succession legally relied exclusively on the male line, although Edward was the closest male relative to the last of his uncles, Charles IV, the crown passed to Philip, who was a cousin to the kings through the male line.

When Philip and Edward came into dispute, the

English king laid claim to the throne of France, refusing to be bound by a French law that had no equivalent in his England. Initially hugely successful, the fortunes of both sides waxed and waned, but a consequence of the period that would become known as the Hundred Years Wars was the unpicking of the close relationship between England and continental Europe, and the emergence of the notion of an English nation.

The English language absorbed many Norman and French words, but it was not until 1484, at the very end of the medieval period, that Parliament first published its laws in the English language. The emergence of an English national identity was an accidental side effect of a fight for a foreign crown. Its birth was slow and stalled at times, but the course initiated by Edward III was never reversed. England was a new nation, raw and proud, and began to consider how it might cease to serve French masters and become not only its own master, but the master of others, starting with France.

68. HERALDIC ACHIEVEMENTS AND ABATEMENTS WERE NOT USED BY MEDIEVAL KNIGHTS

Heraldry was a vital part of medieval chivalry, tournament and warfare. A coat of arms identified a man of status and wearing his livery marked out his men-at-arms on the battlefield. Heralds were the arbitrators of medieval battle, impartial referees who were required to officially decide upon the victor. Although they would accompany their master it was understood on all sides that they were above the fighting and effectively neutral.

Heraldic achievements and abatements are elements of heraldry that seems to draw uncertainty about their existence. Achievements were supposedly granted in recognition of a great service to the crown and abatements denoted some failure of honour or misdemeanour. However, any references to the nature and use of achievements appear after the medieval period, referring back to incidents that do not appear in contemporary chronicles.

The first mention of a heraldic abatement appears in a contemporary document entitled Tractatus de Armis, written by Johannes de Bado Aureo at the request of Anne of Bohemia, first wife of Richard II, at the end of the fourteenth century. Johannes prescribed that the punishment for acts of cowardice, breach of promise or gross misconduct was for the offender to suffer the shame of having their coat of arms displayed either upside down, or reversed. There are references to this punishment being used in cases of treason. When Hugh Despenser the Younger, an unpopular favourite of Edward II, was executed in 1326 he was tied to a horse and forced to wear a tabard of his own coat of arms reversed.

Lists of other abatements include marks placed on a coat of arms for lying to a sovereign, drunkenness, adultery, cowardice, killing a prisoner who has asked for quarter, boasting of a deed not in fact done and revoking a challenge that has been issued. The principle states that a certain cover would be applied to the coat of arms until some positive act redeemed the offender. As heraldry moved from practical use to the show of tournaments the legend of these abatements seems to have emerged and become accepted with no real evidence of any but the reversal of arms.

Heraldic achievements appear to be as much a myth as abatements. There is a story of Edward I's grant of an achievement to a particularly efficient tax collector, but it was not recorded until the Tudor era over two hundred years later.

It seems likely that heraldic achievements and abatements are a later embellishment to the field of heraldry. Although the reversal of arms was prescribed and recorded as being used, no evidence supports the existence of other abatements or achievements during the medieval era.

69. Oxford's Town and Gown Divide Has a Long History

Relations between the town of Oxford and the university authorities have been sour for centuries. Trouble was brewing in the town for years and in 1355 it came to a violent head that irrevocably scarred the relationship.

In 1209 an episode took place that was later recorded by Roger of Wendover. An Oxford student accidentally killed a woman and in his panic he fled the town and could not be found. In an act of extreme vengeance the mayor and the city officials seized the student's three roommates and hanged them. In response to the outrage many masters, clerks and students left Oxford and set up a rival university at Cambridge.

The tense relationship between town and gown continued over the following decades, with frequent outbreaks of violence. It came to a head in devastating fashion on St Scholastica's Day, 10 February 1355. A group of students were drinking in the Swindlestock Tavern when they began to complain to the landlord, John Barford, who also happened to be the mayor of the town, about the quality of the ale. The argument became heated and a tankard was thrown at the landlord, hitting him on the head.

Barford headed straight to St Martin's Church and rang the bells to summon the townsfolk. In response, the students charged to the university's church at St Mary's and rang their bells to call the student body out to fight. The students had the upper hand that evening, but the following day Barford rode out to the surrounding countryside and returned with around 2,000 men. They streamed into the town shouting, 'Havoc! Havoc! Smyte!' and a full-blown riot ensued.

By the end of the fighting thirty townsmen were dead and sixty-three students had been killed. Edward III ordered an investigation which found that the fault lay with the town. The university's privileges were restated and extended and the townsfolk were punished for their part in the riot. The mayor and town bailiffs were ordered to walk through the town each St Scholastica's Day to attend a Mass for the dead of 1355. They had to swear an oath recognising the university's privileges and pay a fine of sixty-three pence, one penny for each student killed.

Every year the town officials were harried and jeered as they paraded through the town. The ritual took place every year until 1825, when the mayor finally refused to undergo the humiliation. The university did not object and the tradition was ended after more than 450 years. To this day the divide between town and gown remains, and there is a saying that 'there are historic battlefields on which less blood has been spilt than in the streets of Oxford'.

70. THE PEASANTS' REVOLT THREATENED A REPUBLICAN REVOLUTION IN ENGLAND

When Edward III died in 1377 the country was at war with France and suffering from poor management that had developed during the king's final years. Justly regarded as a perfect exemplar of medieval kingship, Edward III is perhaps the father of the English national identity, but a series of strokes left him unable to rule in his final years. At his death he was succeeded by his ten-year-old grandson, Richard II, whose father, the Black Prince, pre-deceased Edward III. In 1381 a group of the lower classes of south-east England organised themselves and marched on London to have their grievances heard.

There were various causes of the Peasants' Revolt. The third poll tax in four years was levied, an unprecedented level of taxation that hit the poorest hard to fund a failing war across the Channel. The unwillingness, or inability, to pay is sharply demonstrated by the drop in around one-third of the adult population appearing on the 1381 returns for the poll tax compared to the 1377 returns. Progressively harsher tax collection methods caused increasing resentment. The people also sought an end to serfdom, a system of enforced labour implemented by a landlord – often the Church – for no pay and leaving less time for the peasants' own work. The Black Death had decimated the population and increased the demand for labour, which was now in short supply. The government legislated to prevent movement of workers and to keep wages low.

On 12 June 1381 a large group of peasants gathered at Mile End to the east of London and on the following morning poured into Southwark and across

London Bridge, targeting those they believed to be behind the poll tax. Simon Sudbury, the Archbishop of Canterbury and Lord Chancellor, was dragged from the Tower of London and beheaded. His skull is still kept at St Gregory's Church in Sudbury, Suffolk, and has undergone facial reconstruction.

Richard II, still just fourteen, arranged to meet the rebels in person at Smithfield on 15 June, in part to cause them to leave London. As Richard and the peasants' representative, Wat Tyler, rode toward each other to speak, the Mayor of London lunged at Tyler with a knife and killed him. There were rumours that Tyler had been disrespectful to the king or had reached for a weapon, but it is unclear precisely why Tyler was killed. His men prepared to attack, but Richard rode across the field to them and offered himself as their captain and champion if they would follow him, promising them freedom.

Many left happy and returned home to burn records of landholding and proof of serfdom as the king had permitted. They would later be executed for these acts when Richard's promises failed to materialise, but throughout the uprising the rebels remained clear about one thing: they were loyal to their king. It was the men in between that they wanted removed, not the monarch.

71. THE SAVOY PALACE WAS LOOTED AND DESTROYED DURING THE PEASANTS' REVOLT

In 1246 Henry III granted a piece of prime London real estate between the Strand and the River Thames, with waterfront access, to the uncle of his wife, Eleanor. Peter, Count of Savoy, was supposedly required to submit three barbed arrows to Henry's Exchequer each year in return for the property. Eleanor was a beautiful woman but quickly became unpopular because of the large number of family members, known as the Savoyards, who accompanied her to England, securing some of the most important positions at court.

Peter built a stunning palace on the edge of the Thames, reputed to be the finest noble home in London. Henry also created him Earl of Richmond. Queen Eleanor eventually purchased the palace and gave it as a gift to her second son, Edmund, Earl of Lancaster, younger brother of Edward I. At that point the palace became a part of the honour of Lancaster and was parcelled with that earldom.

When John, King of France, was captured by the Black Prince, oldest son of Edward III, at the Battle of Poitiers in 1357, he was lodged in the Savoy Palace. In 1360 his ransom was set at three-million crowns and he was released to raise the money, his second son, Louis, acting as a hostage in Calais. The money proved hard to raise and in 1363 Louis escaped. To the dismay of the French people John took ship to England to surrender himself, his honour affronted by his son's actions. He took up residence at the Savoy Palace again, dying there on 9 April 1364.

Eventually the Savoy Palace passed to John of Gaunt, third son of Edward III, who had become

Earl of Lancaster by marriage, later becoming Duke of Lancaster. In 1377 John was becoming deeply unpopular in London because of his support for John Wycliffe, leader of the Lollard movement of religious reformers who were considered heretics. Londoners threatened to demolish the Savoy Palace in protest but the Bishop of London managed to restrain them.

When the Peasants' Revolt arrived in London in 1381 the Savoy was a prime target. John now shouldered much of the blame for the unpopular poll tax that sparked the rebellion. The Savoy was set alight after being filled with gunpowder to ensure total demolition. Looting, though, was not the aim. All jewellery and valuables were collected, smashed and thrown into the raging fire. Any that escaped the flames were tossed into the river. Several men had found the wine cellar and became trapped within as the palace burned. One man was allegedly killed by his colleagues for trying to steal a silver cup.

The Savoy remained a ruin for over a century until it was rebuilt as a hospital by Henry VII. The Savoy Hotel today stands on the spot once occupied by this jewel of London's townhouses, where political protest overrode greed.

72. RICHARD II WAS THE FIRST TO INSIST UPON BEING CALLED 'YOUR MAJESTY'

Royal titles were traditionally used to refer to an attribute of the monarch worthy of praise. It is widely believed that the term 'Your Majesty' did not come into use until the sixteenth century when Henry VIII adopted it. Whilst it may have been his favourite term of address, it was in wide use for over a century before the reign of the second Tudor monarch.

Richard II first insisted on being addressed as either 'Highness' or 'Majesty' in the late fourteenth century, as part of his bid to add a golden sheen to his kingship and set himself even further apart from other men. Prior to Richard's reign kings were generally happy to be addressed as 'my Lord', but this form of address also applied to barons and earls. Richard believed that he should stand apart from and clearly above all of these people.

Richard II had a vision of kingship as divine: appointed by and therefore preferred by God. When he sat in state on a raised dais he would cast his eyes about the court and if his eyes settled on a person they were required to fall to their knees and bow to the king for as long as his gaze rested upon them. By the last few years of the fourteenth century Richard's rule was descending into tyranny, as he sought vicious revenge upon those who had tried to restrain him earlier in his reign. He was unseated in 1399 by his cousin Henry IV, the first Lancastrian king, but his ideal of a more regal, lofty kingship remained.

By 1483 'Your Majesty' appears to have been as widely used as 'Your Highness' and 'Your Grace'. When Rhys ap Thomas sent an oath to the new king,

Richard III, promising to prevent an invasion of his kingdom, Thomas wrote, 'Whoever ill-affected to the state shall dare to land in those parts of Wales where I have employment under your majesty, must resolve with himself to make his irruption over my belly.'

The development of new, more exalted forms of address reflected the progress of the monarchy, as well as the monarchs' image of themselves and the institution they represented during the medieval period. The king moved from being the greatest among equals, referred to by their title of 'My Lord', to being a semi-deified figure requiring a higher form of deference. Richard II began this transformation of lordship into majesty and the title perhaps became most associated with Henry VIII because he was the Early Modern embodiment of the same medieval notion expounded by Richard II.

73. HALLOWEEN HAD ITS ORIGINS IN THE MEDIEVAL CELEBRATION OF A PAGAN FESTIVAL

When the early Christian Church was spreading across Europe it sought to convert all those it found, many of whom were pagan. In order to make the assimilation of Christendom smoother and more appealing, the Church set many of its most important religious festivals to coincide with those of the pagan calendar.

Samhain was a festival that marked the end of summer and the beginning of winter. It was the point in the year when crops were gathered and safely stored for the winter. 31 October represented a threshold in the year and it was believed that the boundaries between the lands of the living and the realm of the dead grew thin, fragile enough to be crossed. It was a time when it was possible to communicate with loved ones who had passed to the other side.

The Christian Church adopted this festival as All Hallows' Eve on 31 October, followed by All Saints' Day on 1 November and All Souls' Day on 2 November. The belief that spirits could enter the world of the living persisted, as did the belief that fire and noise confused them and caused them to pass by. All Hallows' Eve became a night of huge bonfires, loud music, dancing and strange masks used to confuse evil spirits.

Soul Cakes were traditionally given to friends and neighbours in return for prayers for deceased loved ones, constituting an early version of the Hallowe'en tradition of trick or treat. Those joining in are part of centuries of rich cultural, social and religious heritage.

74. THE FIRST REFORMATION WAS ENGLISH

John Wycliffe was born in Yorkshire around 1330 and received a superb education at Oxford University before taking up several minor posts in the Church. Whilst working in these posts he continued to study at Oxford, becoming a Bachelor of Divinity in 1369 and receiving his doctorate in 1372. A couple of years later Wycliffe came to the attention of the king, Edward III, who added him to a diplomatic mission to Bruges to resolve several longstanding issues with the papacy. Wycliffe was hailed for staunchly advocating the king's cause and the trip seems to have left a political mark on Wycliffe too.

Wycliffe wrote of his beliefs on the divine in *De domino divino libri tres* and of his more temporal opinions in *Tracatus de civil dominio*. The views that he expressed were explosive. Wycliffe believed that an individual's pious life was more important than religious office. He wrote that the Church should divest itself of all its worldly power and wealth and return to preaching from poverty. Wycliffe then extended this principle to the monarch.

As Wycliffe preached, with some sympathy, in London, he came to the attention of John of Gaunt, third son of Edward III, who was himself at odds with the Church and saw in Wycliffe a useful weapon. This union caused concern amongst Wycliffe's superiors and he was summoned before an enquiry. John of Gaunt applied significant pressure on Wycliffe's behalf and nothing came of the proceedings.

Returning to his studies, Wycliffe began to focus on the doctrine of transubstantiation during Mass: the accepted belief that bread and wine were physically transformed into the body and blood of Christ during the ceremony. Wycliffe instead contended that they remained bread and wine, refusing to accept that they were utterly destroyed and replaced, insisting instead that the bread and wine remained but that Christ was present in an ethereal form. Along with this belief Wycliffe launched a savage attack on the clergy and those in religious orders. A group known as the Lollards began to follow Wycliffe's teachings and were increasingly militant, though it is unclear quite how involved Wycliffe himself was with them.

In 1380 John began to translate the Bible into English, convinced that every man had the right to read the word of God and that reading and developing an interpretation of the Bible was the surest way to understanding how to attain salvation. Wycliffe may have personally translated the whole of the New Testament whilst employing others to translate the Old Testament. His Bible was completed by 1382, when the new Archbishop of Canterbury, William Courtenay, had Wycliffe's teachings banned.

John Wycliffe died in 1384 after a series of strokes and is frequently viewed as the forerunner of the Protestant Reformation. Many of his views were later mirrored in Luther's teachings. The Reformation almost took hold in England some one hundred and forty years before it blazed across Europe.

75. RICHARD II COMMISSIONED THE FIRST COOKBOOK

The *Forme of Cury* is a set of recipes gathered together in 1390 by the master cooks of Richard II. A grandson of the mighty Edward III, Richard had come to the throne at the age of ten in 1377. By 1390 he was a young man of twenty-three, ruling in his own right and keen to stamp his personality and his authority on his court and kingdom.

Unfortunately, Richard's personality was to prove his undoing and his brand of authority was unpalatable to his nobles. He had been restrained by powerful nobles in the mid-1380s in parliaments known as the Wonderful Parliament and the Merciless Parliament. Politically hemmed in, Richard expressed himself through the finery and lavish opulence of his court.

Clothing and ceremony played an important role, but food was another way in which wealth and power could be displayed to all at court. The royal kitchens were staffed exclusively by men because they commanded higher wages, and so employing them displayed the king's wealth in a conspicuous manner. Food was a weapon of power and control, and Richard II was in need of all the weapons he could find.

In 1390 the king's master cooks compiled a vast compendium of recipes used in the royal kitchens. The book was entitled *Forme of Cury* and drew together some of the most prestigious recipes of the late fourteenth century. Spices, imported at great cost, include those familiar to us now, such as cloves, pepper, nutmeg and ginger, and some not so well known, including galangal, cebubs, grains of paradise and maces.

The recipes contained within *Forme of Cury* include now obscure delicacies such as mortrews, a dish of ground and spiced pork and blank mang, which consists of meat sweetened with milk, sugar and almonds. The instructions for Payn Fondew described frying bread in oil or grease, soaking it in red wine and adding raisins and honey with salt and spices.

Forme of Cury is believed to be one of the earliest surviving examples of what we would refer to today as a recipe book. It was a signal of Richard's power, but also of his refinement. It is believed that he personally invented the cloth handkerchief to use at table and was the first to make use of a spoon. His architectural legacy includes the hammer-beam roof of Westminster Hall that can be seen today. As much as any of these other things, the collection of recipes presented to him was a mark of his power and his authority and a measure of his wealth, designed for all to see and marvel at.

76. Henry V Was Scarred for Life

Prince Henry was the oldest son of Henry IV, the first Lancastrian king. Henry IV suffered years of rebellions and unrest after seizing the throne from Richard II. Prince Henry was just sixteen when he took the field at the Battle of Shrewsbury on 21 July 1403 and he was to receive an injury that would scar him for life and perhaps define the course of a kingdom.

The Percy family, the earls of Northumberland, were in open rebellion against Henry IV and had marched south to offer battle. The two armies faced each other near Shrewsbury in July, and during one of the volleys of missile fire the young Prince Harry was struck in the face by an arrow, which buried itself six inches into his right cheek at a downward angle. The Percy army was defeated, the famous Harry Hotspur falling during the fighting, and the young prince was rushed away for medical treatment.

The shaft of the arrow was removed but the barbed head remained firmly lodged in the prince's cheek. The London surgeon John Bradmore was eventually summoned and he later wrote of the treatment he gave in a book entitled *Philomena*, describing the method he used to remove the arrow head.

> First, I made small probes from the pith of an elder, well dried and well stitched in purified linen [made to] the length of the wound. These probes were infused with rose honey. And after that, I made larger and longer probes, and so I continued to always enlarge these probes until I had the width and depth of the wound as I wished it. And after the wound was as enlarged and deep enough so that, by my reckoning, the probes

reached the bottom of the wound, I prepared anew some little tongs, small and hollow, and with the width of an arrow. A screw ran through the middle of the tongs, whose ends were well rounded both on the inside and outside, and even the end of the screw, which was entered into the middle, was well rounded overall in the way of a screw, so that it should grip better and more strongly.

Bradmore slowly widened the hole and worked the arrowhead free. The gaping hole in the prince's cheek now had to be treated. Bradmore washed the hole out and wiped the inside with a swab covered in honey, barley, flour and flax to act as antiseptics. Every day for the next three weeks, Bradmore cleaned and redressed the wound, applying relaxing medicines to Henry's neck to prevent seizures.

This wound is the reason that Henry V's portrait only shows him in profile from the left. His right cheek was scarred permanently and it is interesting to wonder at the emotional scars left on a sixteen-year-old boy who would later invade and conquer France in pursuit of divine approval and temporal acceptance.

77. Owain Glyndwr Nearly Won an Independent Wales

After taking his cousin's throne in 1399 Henry IV suffered many rebellions and threats to his newly established authority. One of the greatest threats to this still-fragile authority came from Wales and one of that nation's greatest legends, Owain Glyndwr. Glyndwr lived just a mile or so from the English border at Sycharth. He could trace both his father's and mother's line back to ancient Welsh royal families, and as these lines began to wither Glyndwr became the focus of attention in the late fourteenth century as the legitimate heir to the proud heritage of the Welsh princes.

When Henry Bolingbroke, who was Earl of Derby and also Lord of Brecon, Kidwelly, Monmouth and Ogmore in Wales, took the throne it created unease in Wales. It was a dispute with a neighbour, Reginald Grey of Ruthin, that seems to have been the spark for Glyndwr's revolt when he could not obtain what he considered to be justice from the new king.

At Glyndyfrdwy a group of his followers proclaimed him Prince of Wales, believing that the time was ripe to push the destabilised English out of Wales and Glyndwr was the man to do it. Although Glyndwr's date of birth is unknown he is believed to have been between thirty and forty by this time. He initiated a campaign of guerrilla warfare, his men attacking English properties and then vanishing into the mist.

Two years later, in 1402, another family of Welsh-noble descent sparked renewed conflict when two brothers, Rhys and Gwilym ap Tudur, along with several other men, executed an audacious plot to capture Conwy Castle, succeeding and holding it from the English for several months. Their other brother, Maredudd, was the great-grandfather of Henry Tudor, who would become Henry VII. Henry IV launched a furious campaign to subdue the Welsh, but made no headway against their illusive forces. In vengeance, Parliament passed the Penal Code, preventing Welshmen from carrying arms, gathering together or holding office.

In the same year, Glyndwr captured his old foe Reginal Grey, along with Edmund Mortimer, the leading alternative claimant to the English throne. When Henry refused to allow Edmund to ransom himself, Edmund married one of Glyndwr's daughters and joined his cause. In 1404 Glyndwr captured Aberystwyth and Harlech Castles before holding a parliament at Machynlleth, where he may have been crowned as Prince of Wales. Glyndwr sought alliance with the King of France, offering to side with him in a dispute over the papacy in return for concessions that amounted to Welsh independence. He requested an archbishopric at St David's, the establishment of two Welsh universities and for clerics to use the Welsh language.

Setbacks began to hinder Glyndwr's campaign. French support was sporadic at best. Henry IV's son, the future Henry V, cut his military teeth recapturing Aberystwyth and Harlech. His cause in tatters, Glyndwr melted into the mist of the Welsh hills. When, where and how he died is a mystery, but his legend lives on today.

78. War Cries Were Dangerous and Tightly Controlled

'Cry havoc! And let slip the dogs of war!' is a famous quote from Shakespeare's Julius Caesar, but the phrase to 'cry havoc' had its origins on the medieval battlefield. It was one of the most dangerous but welcome battle cries of the medieval English army.

'Montez' was a call given instructing all those who were able to mount, leading to the breaking of ranks. The breach of discipline and formation that it might cause could be catastrophic, meaning it was a potentially dangerous instruction to give in error or at the wrong time.

The most heavily regulated cry on the battlefield was 'havoc' and the control of this order features strongly in Ordinances drawn up for medieval English armies. A call of havoc freed the army from their formation and gave them permission to fall to pillage, gathering whatever money and valuable prisoners they might be able to find. It was the signal that the battle was won and the spoils could be taken.

A wrongly timed cry of havoc would undermine the structure of the army and cause chaos, possibly costing a commander the battle. For this reason havoc was a tightly regulated call, given only by the most senior commanders present. Anyone crying havoc without permission would be severely punished. Frequently the defined fate was beheading. Such was the danger of crying havoc and letting slip the dogs of war too soon.

79. THE BATTLE OF AGINCOURT WAS A HOLLOW VICTORY

In pouring rain and the thick, sucking mud of a field between the towns of Azincourt and Tramecourt, on St Crispin's Day, 25 October 1415, a bedraggled band of English archers and men-at-arms formed ranks behind their king to fight a vast army that boasted the flower of French chivalry and nobility. The odds were not in their favour, yet they famously won the day. The battle, though, altered little in the short term. So why was Agincourt so important?

Henry V had sailed from Southampton on 11 August 1415 with a huge fleet and a vast army. He laid siege to Harfleur, during which the French army was conspicuous by its absence. Charles VI of France suffered from mental instability and his eighteen-year-old son, Louis, the Dauphin (the French heir apparent, equivalent to the Prince of Wales), was left to organise France's response to Henry's invasion. Louis was a stark contrast to Henry V, who was a paragon of impeccable martial etiquette and achievement. When Henry sent Louis a personal challenge to one-to-one combat for the crown of France, Louis did not even reply.

After the siege of Harfleur the English army left a garrison in the town and the remainder, their numbers reduced by dysentery, were to head for Calais, the only other enclave of English territory on the Continent. Rather than sail along the coast, Henry decided to provocatively march his men right through France, intending to cross the Somme at the same point that his great-grandfather Edward III had in 1346, before Crécy.

Only now did the French army move, though it was not under the leadership of Louis. French chivalry would stomach the affront no longer. They shadowed Henry's army, trying to prevent them from crossing the Somme and force a confrontation. A challenge was issued to Henry to name a date and field to give battle. Henry replied that there was no need, since he was in the open all day every day and ready to fight whenever and wherever they wished.

At Agincourt they finally met. Estimates suggest Henry had between 6,000 and 9,000 men left. The French had between 12,000 and 36,000. It rained heavily during the night of 24 October and the armies rose to a quagmire separating them. Henry used this to his advantage and ordered spikes to be driven into the earth to prevent cavalry charges. Somehow the English won the day, losing only about 100 men to around 7–10,000 French casualties, with some notable lords captured and taken back to England.

The Battle of Agincourt changed little in October 1415. Henry made it to Calais and returned to England having only gained Harfleur. The true impact of Agincourt came when Henry returned to France, as the battle had all but wiped out the French ruling classes and military leadership. France had been rendered incapable of effective defence, and this facilitated the greatest period of conquest on French soil in English history.

80. Henry V's Ordinances Kept His Army Disciplined

The campaigns of Henry V that culminated on 21 May 1420 with the signing of the Treaty of Troyes, which recognised Henry as the legal heir to the throne of Charles VI of France, are legendary. Henry's attitude to his men and to his enemies has remained a hotly contested issue. To some, he was a strict but fair leader, capable of unrivalled inspiration. Others, though, see his actions as vicious and a cruel means to an end. Either way, discipline was his watchword.

After his teenage years Henry V had cast aside frivolity almost at the moment of becoming king in 1413, when he sent all of the friends of his misspent youth away from him with thanks for their company and a request never to return. By 1415 he had won the famous victory at Agincourt and was soon back in France to make the most of the gains that he had made.

The Statutes of Ordinances of the Army prescribed by Henry in 1419 remain extant and demonstrate not only how closely he defined what was acceptable behaviour, but also how little was new about the methods that he employed. The 1419 Ordinances bear a strong similarity to those created in 1386 by Richard II.

The first instruction was an unequivocal requirement for loyalty to the king, his constable and his marshall. The next two prohibited the violation of churches. The only soldier recorded as punished during the Agincourt campaign was hanged for stealing a pyx from a church. Assuming that the Ordinances were the same as those drawn up in 1419, he would have known his fate if he was caught.

Several articles dealt with the maintaining of watches and keeping men within their units. The king was to be permitted to call a muster at will to inspect the troops and any man found outside his own unit was to be punished. All soldiers were to wear a large and clearly visible cross of St George to identify them as Englishmen.

Those who cried havoc in battle, gave battle without the king's leave, plundered towns or villages that had already been conquered or had surrendered, attacked women or left the army without leave could expect firm punishment.

The taking of prisoners was also carefully provided for. Anyone who knocked an enemy to the ground had first rights to the prisoner. He was responsible for the care of that prisoner, for presenting him to the king, constable or marshall and for giving one-third of any bounty to the lord who led his force.

However Henry V might be viewed, he was clear about the requirement for discipline. It is perhaps telling that only one man was hanged during the entire Agincourt campaign. Henry's rules worked because everyone was aware of what they were and were not permitted to do and what punishment awaited any breach. Those who chose to break them knew the risk they took.

81. Dick Whittington Made His Fortune Without His Cat

Dick Whittington is one of Britain's most famous pantomimes. The poor young Dick travels to London in search of his fortune, living in an attic with his cat, who kept the mice away. When Dick becomes disillusioned he sells his cat to a ship's captain and prepares to return home. As he is leaving, the bells chime for him to return, promising that he will thrice be Lord Mayor of London. It transpires that his cat was the hero of a voyage and Dick becomes rich. It is perhaps surprising how much of this tale is true and how much of the truth about Dick Whittington has been forgotten.

Richard Whittington was born in the 1350s, a younger son of Sir William Whittington, Lord of the Manor of Pauntley in Gloucestershire. Richard's father died in 1358 and, with all of the inheritance going to his older brother, Richard decided to head to London in search of his fortune. This portion of the story is true, then, except that Richard, as the son of a lord, was never really all that poor.

After serving his apprenticeship Richard became a mercer, trading in valuable cloths such as velvet and silk. As a supplier to the sumptuous court of Richard II, business was good and Dick grew very wealthy, frequently lending money to the Crown. When the Lord Mayor of London died in 1397 the king appointed Dick Whittington to the post and he was elected again the following year. When Richard II was deposed in 1199 he owed Dick Whittington £1,000.

Dick's good relations with the crown continued under Henry IV, as he lent money to the new Lancastrian regime and he served a third term as mayor in 1406. Growing wealthier by the year, Dick became a vital part of Henry V's military campaigns as a willing provider of funds. Shortly after Henry V became king, Dick loaned him £2,000, and when the siege of Harfleur, the first action of the Agincourt campaign, took longer than envisaged, Dick Whittington was among the wealthy London merchants who loaned more money to the king. Dick himself forwarded £700, and this steadfast service possibly contributed to Dick's re-election as Mayor of London in 1419 for the fourth time.

During his lifetime Dick was something of a philanthropist, creating a ward within St Thomas's Hospital for unmarried mothers, rebuilding the Guildhall and opening a public toilet with 128 seats. On his death in his seventies in 1423, Richard Whittington left no children. His vast fortune established a library at the Guildhall, funded an almshouse and hospital for the poor, rebuilt Newgate Prison and created public drinking fountains.

Today, the Whittington Charity still supports those in need, with gifts distributed by the Mercer Company. Sometimes, the truth is even more amazing than fiction.

82. THERE WERE MANY DIFFERENT
RELIGIOUS ORDERS IN MEDIEVAL BRITAIN

The medieval period saw the growth of religious orders across Europe. They became vast landowners and powerful members of society, driving trade and helping the poor. At the height of their power they acted as schools, hospitals and moral centres. At their best they were the medieval equivalent of the welfare state. It is hard to pinpoint a time and reason for their decline, but for every good monastery there was a bad one, meaning that the reverse was true too.

Throughout the medieval era there were many different brands of religious order, each with a different approach to achieving their shared aim. Perhaps the most famous group was the Benedictine order, founded by St Benedict in AD 529. Benedictines took vows of poverty, obedience, chastity and labour, the last of which required them to complete seven hours of manual labour every day. Benedictine Abbeys can be found at Glastonbury, Dunfermline and Iona.

Cluniacs arrived in Britain at Lewes shortly after the Norman Conquest. A branch of the Benedictine Order, they preached a return to the original rules of St Benedict, which had become altered by the main trunk of the Benedictine order. Cluniac monasteries are found at Much Wenlock and Thetford.

In 1221 the Black Friars arrived at Oxford. Following the teachings of St Dominic, their rule was harsh and strict, requiring absolute poverty and prolonged periods of fasting, even from drink. Over the following centuries they spread throughout Britain.

Grey Friars were followers of St Francis of Assisi. The Friars Minor, as they are also called, took up St

Francis's teachings that complete poverty was required by the Gospels and was the only way to serve God. The first Grey Friars establishment was founded at Canterbury in 1224 and by the end of the medieval period they had become established in Edinburgh and many other towns and cities where they worked to support the poor.

Augustinians, or Black Canons, arrived in Britain in the eleventh century. They became very popular and their establishments were large and wealthy because of their commitment to reaching out to the communities around them. They went out to preach within local communities and were generous with alms giving.

In contrast to the Augustinians, the Cistercian Order established themselves in remote, rural locations, often in Wales and northern England. With a strong focus on farming and working the land, they became, almost inadvertently, very wealthy. Fountains Abbey is a fine example of their gothic architecture.

Carthusians were an extremely harsh order. Members spent six days a weeks alone in their cells wearing hair shirts. Their hard rules and reclusive lifestyle meant that they were isolated from the communities that surrounded them.

The Knights Templar and Knights Hospitallar were military orders, combining martial responsibilities with religious devotion. When the Templars were disbanded the Hospitallars took over much of their lands, including Temple Church in London.

83. Sir John Fastolf Was Suspended from the Order of the Garter for Cowardice

Medieval orders of chivalry were widespread across Europe, frequently founded for a noble aim or for a limited time to achieve an end, some requiring the member to perform specific tasks or pay a fee. One of the most famous and longest surviving chivalric orders is the Order of the Garter, founded in 1344 by Edward III. The results and implications of Sir John Falstaff's suspension from the Order demonstrate how seriously chivalry and honour were taken in the late medieval period.

The Order of the Garter was created by Edward III around the time that he laid claim to the throne of France. The order was, and still is, comprised of the monarch, the Prince of Wales and twenty-four Companions. Originally these were two tournament teams of thirteen, one led by the king and the other by his heir, and the teams lined stalls opposite each other in St George's Chapel, Windsor.

Edward III gave the order the motto *Honi soit qui mal y pense*, which translates from the French as 'shame on he who thinks ill of it'. Although the exact origins of this motto are uncertain, it has been suggested that it relates to Edward's claim to the French throne and his determination to prove it. Chivalry and honour were at the heart of the Order of the Garter and so sanctions were designed to remove those who violated any part of the code of chivalry.

In 1429 France was resurgent against the occupying English, led by Joan of Arc, and the culmination of this renewed conflict came on 18 June 1429 at the Battle of

Patay. A smaller French force conclusively crushed the English army, who suffered over 2,000 casualties. John Talbot, who was later created Earl of Shrewsbury, was captured at Patay and remained a prisoner in France for four years. Sir John Fastolf had led a portion of the army but escaped.

On securing his release, Talbot immediately accused Fastolf of cowardice and he was suspended from the Order of the Garter pending an investigation. Henry VI's uncle and regent, John, Duke of Bedford, led the investigation and eventually found no fault in Fastolf's actions, reinstating him as a member of the order.

That was not the end of the matter. Talbot and Fastolf remained at odds for years. John Fastolf retained the services of a secretary, William Worcester, for twelve years, to lead the compilation of a legal defence to the charges that Talbot persisted in repeating. Eventually another inquiry was held in 1442 at which Fastolf was finally exonerated.

Sir John Fastolf was to become the basis of Shakespeare's famous comedic coward Sir John Falstaff. Honour was everything to a medieval knight, worth fighting for decades to preserve. Cleared in his lifetime, Fastolf has nevertheless lost his immense achievements to comedy. He would surely be distraught.

84. Henry VI Is the Only Person Ever Crowned King of England and France

Henry VI ruled England from 1421 to 1461 and from 1470 to 1471. He holds a unique position in medieval British history as the only monarch to be crowned king of both England and France.

By the late 1420s the conquests in France made by Henry VI's father, Henry V, were in danger. France was regrouping and growing resurgent. Henry V had negotiated the Treaty of Troyes before his death, which nominated him and his successors as the legitimate heirs to the throne of France. Charles VI of France died within months of Henry V, making the infant Henry VI king of both England and France at the age of nine months.

The son of Charles VI was crowned King of France in 1429 and Henry's government saw a danger in allowing Charles VII the prestige of an unopposed coronation, but the young Henry had not yet been crowned King of England. The council swiftly arranged the seven-year-old Henry's coronation and on 6 November 1429 at Westminster Abbey he underwent the arduous ordeal of the coronation ceremony, bearing up remarkably well for such a young child, as he was prostrated before the altar, stripped, anointed with holy oil and redressed in his royal regalia.

On 23 April 1430, St George's Day, Henry and the cream of the English nobility set sail for Calais. The young king's progress was slow. The intention was to perform his coronation in Paris, but as the French grew in confidence Paris became less and less secure. Henry remained at Rouen, the capital city of Normandy, for sixteen months before moving on towards the French capital. On 16 December 1431, after witnessing a breath-taking display of pageantry as he entered the city, Henry, now just passed his tenth birthday, underwent another coronation ceremony at Notre Dame Cathedral. The Bishop of Paris, in whose cathedral the ceremony was conducted, was doubtless put out when the king's great-uncle Henry Beaufort, Cardinal Bishop of Winchester, insisted upon performing the ceremony himself.

Henry remained in Paris for less than a week. The feast that followed his coronation was not well received, and there were complaints that no local merchants had profited from the affair in spite of putting on a lavish show at a poor time of year and in a difficult period for the city. Both ceremonies had been adapted to emphasise the unique nature of the days, but in trying to please everyone it seems that all were left wanting.

Henry's time in France, with its deified view of monarchy, left a lasting mark on the young boy. For almost a century English kings had claimed the crown of France. Only one man has ever worn both and he would find himself unable to retain either.

85. MEDIEVAL NOBLES DEVELOPED A TASTE FOR MACABRE TOMBS

Toward the end of the medieval period a fashion emerged amongst the elite of the Church and the nobility for visceral, gory tomb effigies that can appear disturbing. Cadaver tombs and transi tombs became all the rage, offering a moral lesson to those looking on, but perhaps more concerned with the soul of the departed than those left behind.

Death was a central part of life in the Middle Ages. Death rates were high and life expectancy lower than today, though high infant mortality dragged down average life expectancy statistics. If a person made it to their teens they might reasonably expect to live to be sixty, barring war, famine and disease! Death was everywhere and was viewed as the great leveller, for even the richest and most powerful could not escape it. The real preoccupation lay in what came next. Life was simply an audition for a place in Heaven. Failure did not bear contemplation.

Cadaver tombs first appeared on the Continent, perhaps in the wake of the Black Death, but the first recorded example in Britain was made for Bishop Richard Fleming at Lincoln Cathedral. The style that became popular in Britain are called transi tombs and are frequently on two levels. At the top of the tomb is a more traditional effigy, recognisable throughout the Middle Ages, of the deceased in full regalia, be it religious robes, noble finery or knightly armour. This represented the person in life, as they wished to be remembered, and was in line with hundreds of years of tradition.

Transi tombs, though, hold a second layer below,

open for all to see, that represents the tomb's inhabitant as they would appear within their sealed coffin. The cadaver effigy is frequently shocking, showing a corpse in the late stages of decomposition with taught, broken skin, visible bones and even maggots or vermin eating the body. So why would someone pay to be shown in this way?

There was a moral element for the viewer. Death could not be evaded by anyone and in the end the rotting cadaver was the inescapable fate of all. In this way, the tombs acted as a memento mori: a reminder of death. There was also a perceived benefit to the person enclosed within the tomb. The transi tomb offered them an opportunity to show humility and penitence by displaying all of their finery, but acknowledging that beneath all of that they were just human beings, destined for the same physical fate as everyone else. In offering penitence for their worldly wealth, they hoped to speed their own passage through Purgatory.

Edward IV's will, written in 1475, made provision that he should 'be buried low in the ground, and upon the same a stone be laid and wrought with the figure of Death'. Edward planned an extreme version of the tomb with Death himself above him. Fitting, perhaps, for a king.

86. JOHN, DUKE OF BEDFORD, WAS THE GREATEST KING ENGLAND NEVER HAD

At the age of forty-six, John, Duke of Bedford, died in Rouen, France. His career rivalled that of any king of England and his achievements rival those of his more famous brother, Henry V.

Born in 1389, John was the third son of Henry Bolingbroke, Earl of Derby. Their grandfather was John of Gaunt, Duke of Lancaster, third son of Edward III. The family's fortunes were transformed in 1399 when John's father seized the throne of his cousin, Richard II. Henry had been exiled after falling out with Richard, but when John of Gaunt died Richard seized the vast Lancastrian inheritance for himself, refusing to allow Henry to take possession of his own inheritance.

John's brother became Henry V on their father's death and his martial intentions were clear. John acted as regent in England three times when the king went to France accompanied by John's other older brother Thomas, Duke of Clarence. In 1416 John aided in the relief of the siege of Harfleur and he was in France with his king when Henry died in 1422.

Henry V was ill long enough to write a careful will. His heir was only nine months old and the empire that he had been building in France was fragile. With Thomas already dead, there was only one man Henry would entrust his life's work to. John was made regent of England and France for his infant nephew, though in practise he spent most of his time leading the effort in France, leaving his younger brother Thomas, Duke of Gloucester, as regent in England.

For the next thirteen years John remained committed to his brother's aims and worked tirelessly to increase his nephew's empire. Constantly deprived of men, money and resources, John was not only an excellent general but an accomplished diplomat. His harsh treatment of Joan of Arc is a blot on his copybook, but it succeeded in ending the cult of her French revival by discrediting her as a heretic.

It was John who insisted on the coronation of Henry VI as King of France in 1431 to reinforce the English advances there. However, John could never have foreseen that Henry was to become the very antithesis of his father, and his coronation, since it could not be undone, made the eventual English exit from France an awkward and messy affair.

John was buried at Rouen Cathedral. When the French finally reclaimed that city the country's knights wanted to tear down the duke's memorial, but Louis XI of France prevented them, acknowledging the worth of his erstwhile opponent, reportedly asking his knights

What honour shall it be to us, or to you to break this monument, and to pull out of the ground and take up the dead bones of him, whom in his life, neither my father not your progenitors with all their power, puissance and friends were once able to make fly one foot backward.

87. Marjery Kempe Wrote the First Autobiography in English

The Book of Marjery Kempe is astonishing for many reasons. It makes for fascinating reading on many levels. Marjery's memoirs are the first-known autobiography written in English, dictated by Marjery herself and completed in 1438. The book also provides a valuable insight into the life of a medieval middle-class woman at a time when very little is known of such people. Marjery's life, though, was far from ordinary.

Born in the early 1370s, Marjery was the daughter of John Brunham, a mayor of Lyn and prominent, wealthy man of the middling sort. At the age of about twenty Marjery married John Kempe, a man of some means himself. They looked set for a comfortable life in the obscurity of normalcy.

John and Marjery's life was radically altered by Marjery's difficult first pregnancy. After giving birth she suffered a breakdown and became plagued by visions of demons. Her condition did not improve for eight months until finally she had a vision of Jesus Christ and emerged from her torment. Determined to dedicate her life to Christ, Marjery found that the world was in the way. Her husband did not wish to live a life of celibacy and Margaret fell pregnant a further thirteen times, though there is no record of how many of her children survived.

After starting a brewing business that failed miserably, Marjery became more and more certain that God wanted her to turn away from the temporal world. As she began to speak about the visions that she had, Marjery attracted attention, not all of which was friendly. She quickly acquired a reputation as an eccentric woman, her words bordering on heresy.

Marjery left England on a long pilgrimage, eventually reaching Jerusalem after travelling via Rome. In Jerusalem she records that she had many strong and vivid visions in which she talked to Jesus and Mary and felt herself present at biblical events. She also began to cry uncontrollably during church services, a trait that would remain with her for the rest of her life.

On the journey home Marjery became stuck in Rome after giving all of her money to the poor. Eventually her disturbing behaviour became such an embarrassment to the English community in Rome that they gave her the funds to return home. When she arrived back in England Marjery's visions continued and she became the focus of attention, some of which grew increasingly unfriendly. Leaving her husband, she travelled throughout the country. In the North she was arrested for heresy but, supported by the Church, no case could be proven.

Marjery visited important religious sites and people throughout the land. When her husband fell ill she returned to Lyn, though the local priest refused to have her in his congregation because of her disruptive wailing. When her husband and son died Marjery travelled to Germany with her daughter-in-law, then returned home and began to dictate her book, giving us a glimpse of a life less ordinary.

88. Henry VI Founded Eton College

Henry VI's legacy is, in general, a very poor one. He was a nice man: too nice to be a good medieval king. As the son of Henry V he had a lot to live up to, but Henry VI preferred prayer and peace to the war that had gifted him an empire. One legacy remains to the present day, though not in the form Henry might have envisaged.

In 1440 Henry granted a charter creating the King's College of Our Lady of Eton Besides the Thames, known today as Eton College. The last Lancastrian king founded the college to offer free education to seventy boys from poor backgrounds. They were to receive the finest education free of charge before transferring to King's College, Oxford, which Henry founded the following year, 1441.

Around 1447 Henry gifted the college a priceless collection of religious relics that his great-uncle Henry Beaufort, Cardinal Bishop of Winchester, had left the king in his will. Among these was a golden tablet, known as the Tablet of Burboyn, which was reputed to contain some of the blood of Jesus Christ, a fragment of the true cross and other relics of the Virgin Mary, Katherine the Virgin and 'other Martyrs, Confessors and Virgins'.

Many of the college's treasures were confiscated in 1461 when Henry VI lost his throne to the first Yorkist king, Edward IV, and placed instead in St George's Chapel, Windsor, across the river. The fate of the tablet remains unknown.

89. Misericords Allowed Monks to Bend the Rules

Many of the required prayer sessions in medieval monasteries, priories and churches were lengthy affairs. Monks in the choir stalls were required to stand throughout the services. Even for those who weren't old or infirm it could be physically tiring. Being no more than human, the monks found a way to bend the rules and rest their feet.

The monks would stand in choir stalls either side of the church where there were seats for the times when sitting was permitted. When standing was required, these seats had to be folded away. Someone hit upon the bright idea of adding an ornate carving to the bottom of the seat which would be visible when the chair was folded up. Each of these carvings was also given a flat shelf at the top, at just the right height to allow a monk to perch and take the weight off his feet without actually sitting down.

Misericords, as these shelves and accompanying carvings are called, are also referred to as pity seats or mercy seats, and can still be found in many churches to this day. The carvings vary widely in their subject and suggest that some of the carpenters were given free rein to have a bit of fun.

Heraldry plays a part in some misericord art, often denoting a patron. St Laurence's Church in Ludlow shows both the falcon and fetter lock and the white rose emblem of Richard, Duke of York, who frequently used Ludlow as a base. Pagan images, such as the Green Man, mermaids and harpies, are frequently found amongst misericords.

Many misericords tell a little story, perhaps of a

wife beating her husband or a man drinking himself into oblivion. It is uncertain whether these humorous tales poked fun at everyday life, or were meant as a reminder to the monks of the worldly sin from which they were (supposedly) removed, but which they were responsible for curing. Tales from *Aesop's Fables* and other medieval folk tales are also frequently found in misericords.

Misericords can still be found in churches around Britain and they are worth finding. Unravelling the story they tell is as subjective now as it was when they were created, but trying to decipher them can be fun. They are, at least, a reminder of long hours spent in prayer and song – the activity for which those areas were designed. More than that, they act as a reminder that the men who stood there were only human and found ways to bend the rules that made their lives difficult.

90. The Wars of the Roses Between York and Lancaster Began at St Albans

The Wars of the Roses is traditionally viewed as a thirty-year period of civil war between the royal houses of Lancaster and York for the crown of England. As with many flashpoints in history, the true story is not quite so simple.

In 1455 the Lancastrian Henry VI had reigned for thirty-three years. He had overseen the complete loss of all of the territory in France that his father had won. He had allowed factions to rupture the unity of his kingdom unchecked and unfairly favoured some men above others.

Henry was struck by a mystery illness in 1454 which rendered him catatonic. It is possible that he inherited some mental instability from his grandfather, Charles VI of France, known as Charles the Mad. For years Charles's incapacity left France defenceless as the king believed that he was made of glass and would shatter if anyone touched him. He was prone to violent outbursts, but his grandson had the opposite affliction. He was completely unresponsive to the world around him.

During Henry's incapacity his cousin Richard, Duke of York, had been selected by Parliament to act as Lord Protector. York was the figurehead of a faction which opposed that led by Edmund Beaufort, Duke of Somerset, and although Somerset enjoyed the king's favour it was to York who the lords turned in their moment of need. York acquitted himself well, showing that he was more even-handed than many had feared his rule would be in the fractious political atmosphere.

When Henry recovered on Christmas Day 1454

it was regarded as a miracle. York resigned as Lord Protector, but was immediately marginalised again as Somerset stepped back into the position he had occupied before Henry's illness. Nothing had changed. Henry summoned a Great Council at Leicester, but York, the Earl of Salisbury and Salisbury's son the Earl of Warwick were excluded. Fearing that they were about to come under political attack, they gathered an army and intercepted the king's forces as they marched north from London, at St Albans on 22 May.

With the royal army trapped within the town, the party led by York won the day. Edmund Beaufort was killed, as was Henry Percy, Earl of Northumberland. King Henry was wounded in the neck by an arrow and was receiving treatment when York, Salisbury and Warwick burst into the tanner's shop into which he had retreated. The lords fell to their knees and pledged their allegiance to the king.

The First Battle of St Albans was not a fight for the crown of England. It was not really between the Houses of Lancaster and York. In 1455 the battle was for influence over an ineffectual king whose rule was threatening to destroy a nation. If York wanted the crown, he had only to finish that arrow's work in the tanner's workshop.

91. Omens Foretold the Fall of Lancaster

The Wars of the Roses may have begun as a struggle for control of a weak king, but in 1460 the faction that had gathered around Richard, Duke of York, radically altered their tactics. As they did so, two omens seemed to predict the doom of the House of Lancaster.

The Duke of York had served as Protector of the Realm twice during Henry VI's incapacity, but had found himself quickly swept aside when the king recovered. Rather than continuing to try and wrest control of the weak king from his opponents, led by the formidable queen, Margaret of Anjou, and Henry Beaufort, Duke of Somerset, York launched his own bid for the throne, arguing that his claim was stronger than Henry's.

The House of Lancaster was descended from John of Gaunt, third son of Edward III. Henry VI was the third Lancastrian king, following his father Henry V and his grandfather Henry IV. King from the age of nine months, Henry was ill-suited to the state of war his kingdom in France lay in. Trouble abroad meant dissatisfaction at home: less chance for booty abroad meant that unpaid, unruly soldiers flooded back into the ports of the South Coast.

The House of York was descended, through the male line, from Edmund, Duke of York, Edward III's fourth son. However, Richard, Duke of York, could also trace his maternal line from Lionel, Duke of Clarence, the second son of Edward III, whose only daughter, Philippa, had married Edmund Mortimer, 3rd Earl of March. Edmund's son Roger, 4th Earl of March, was the father of Anne Mortimer, who married Richard of

Conisburgh, Earl of Cambridge, second son of Edward, 2nd Duke of York. Anne and Richard were the parents of Richard, 3rd Duke of York, who inherited the title from his uncle Edward, 2nd Duke of York, the most notable Englishman killed at Agincourt.

Richard had served as Lieutenant in France and had acquitted himself well in his terms as Lord Protector, yet he remained marginalised. Treated with suspicion by Margaret of Anjou, it is hard to discern whether her mistrust was well placed, or if it turned out to be a self-fulfilling prophecy.

In 1460, Richard walked into Westminster Hall and laid a hand on the throne, symbolically claiming it. There was silence in the chamber. None cheered and clapped, as Richard may have expected them to. He was asked to present details of his claim to place before Parliament. As Richard spoke, a decorative crown hanging in the Palace of Westminster fell to the ground of its own accord. At the same time, in Dover Castle, a crown also fell from its mount.

Together, the falling of two crowns was taken to be an omen, a signifier of the doom of the House of Lancaster. Perhaps it actually signified the fall of both great houses.

92. THE LARGEST BATTLE ON BRITISH SOIL WAS FOUGHT AT TOWTON ON PALM SUNDAY

The Houses of York and Lancaster had been fighting each other for the crown for two years, with losses and the hunger for revenge raging on both sides. This phase of the civil war reached an apex on Palm Sunday, 29 March 1461, a day which left the country soaked in blood. The battle that was fought at Towton in Yorkshire remains the largest, bloodiest battle ever fought on British soil.

Richard, Duke of York, had been slain at the Battle of Wakefield three months earlier. His eighteen-year-old son, Edward, Earl of March, had laid claim to the throne of Henry VI and gathered an immense army to meet the Lancastrians in the North. He was joined by his key ally, Richard Neville, Earl of Warwick, later known as the Kingmaker. Warwick's huge Neville family had backed the House of York and Warwick's own father, the Earl of Salisbury, had been killed alongside Edward's father and younger brother Edmund, Earl of Rutland.

The Lancastrians had exacted a measure of revenge at the Battle of Wakefield on 30 December 1460. Henry Beaufort, Duke of Somerset, Henry Percy, Earl of Northumberland, and Lord Clifford had all lost fathers at the First Battle of St Albans in 1455 and had been straining at the leash for vengeance ever since. In killing the Duke of York, his second son and the head of the Neville family they had extracted their revenge, but in turn made themselves targets for their enemies.

William Neville, Lord Fauconberg, led the centre of the Yorkist army. Probably the most experienced and respected general in England in his day, Fauconberg was a natural choice. It was a miserable day, snow reducing visibility and biting winds adding to the chill. Fauconberg immediately spied his advantage. With the wind at their backs he ordered his longbowmen to open fire. The arrow storm, driven by the wind, wreaked havoc on the Lancastrian army, who returned fire into the wind but found their enemies out of range. The Yorkists fired all of their arrows, stepped forward to collect the Lancastrian shafts planted in the ground before them and continued loosing arrow after arrow.

The hand-to-hand fighting that followed was close for a long time. Finally, John Mowbray, Duke of Norfolk, arrived with fresh reinforcements for the Yorkists and the sight of them drained the last of the Lancastrian resolve.

Estimates place the number of men on the field at Towton between 60,000 and 100,000. Several accounts give a figure of 29,000 for the number who died in the snow that day, with one reporting 36,000 casualties. One report states that the fighting lasted a gruelling ten hours. The white snow was streaked with red and mass graves were carved out of the frozen ground. Towton destroyed the Lancastrian cause for years and left deep scars across a battered country.

93. THE BATTLE OF NIBLEY GREEN WAS THE LAST PRIVATE BATTLE IN ENGLAND

The Wars of the Roses was reignited in 1469 as the Kingmaker, the Earl of Warwick, came to blows with his former friend Edward IV. As the greatest men in the land aired their grievances, many took the opportunity to resolve long-running disputes of their own. On 20 March 1470 the last battle between private armies on English soil took place in an effort to settle one such argument.

Lord Lisle of Wotton and Lord Berkeley of Berkeley Castle had been involved in a legal dispute over an inheritance for years. Lord Lisle believed that he was entitled to some of the lands held by Lord Berkeley, but progress in the courts was slow and expensive. As the re-emergence of civil war preoccupied the country, Lord Lisle and Lord Berkeley decided to settle the matter themselves.

With less than 1,000 men each they faced each other on the green at North Nibley in Gloucestershire. The early morning fighting was fierce and Lord Berkeley emerged victorious. He later had the south aisle of St Martin's church in North Nibley built to commemorate his victory and many of the men killed that morning are buried in the graveyard of the church.

The Battle of Nibley Green was the last time two private armies met each other in battle to settle a private quarrel. It was a symptom of the wider disorder that was brewing and a testament to the willingness of powerful men to exploit political disruption for their own ends.

94. Only Once Has a King Lost His Crown then Invaded and Regained His Throne

There are two medieval kings of England who lost their throne and were then restored. It is no coincidence that they vied with each other for the crown, nor that their conflict formed a part of the bitter rivalries known as the Wars of the Roses, when the red rose of Lancaster fought with the white rose of York for control of the garden of England.

Henry VI had become king at the age of nine months when his father, Henry V, died in 1422. In 1461 he lost his crown to the eighteen-year-old Duke of York, who became Edward IV. When Edward fell out with some of his most powerful subjects, notably the Earl of Warwick, Henry's continued existence gave them a route to opposition.

In 1470 Edward IV lost his grip on power and was driven into exile in Burgundy for six months, during which Henry VI was wheeled out of the Tower of London, dusted down and reinstated as king. Edward fled England from King's Lynn to the court of his brother-in-law Charles the Bold, Duke of Burgundy. Only six months later he sailed for England to reclaim his crown. Fierce storms raged in the Channel. An attempt to land in Norfolk was beaten back by the Earl of Oxford's men and Edward eventually landed at Ravenspur in Yorkshire, the same spot at which Henry IV had landed when he came to take the throne from Richard II.

Making his way south, he encountered his old friend and mentor Richard Neville, the Kingmaker, at the Battle of Barnet on 14 April 1471. On 4 May he completed his victory at the Battle of Tewkesbury, where Henry VI's only child, the seventeen-year-old Prince Edward of Westminster, Prince of Wales, was killed. On the evening that Edward IV returned to London Henry VI was killed. Although one Yorkist source claims that he died of 'pure displeasure and melancholy' at the news of the loss of his cause, it is likely Edward ordered his death, perhaps at the hands of his brother Richard, Duke of Gloucester. Henry VI may have survived his first deposition because his son was alive and would simply replace Henry as a new, more vigorous and more popular figurehead, but with both the Kingmaker and Henry's heir slain in battle, there was no further need for the old Lancastrian king.

Edward II had lost his throne in 1327 and Richard II was deposed in 1399. Both men never returned to the political scene, though the final fate of both is a matter of some conjecture.

Henry VI was the first king of England to lose his throne and regain it. Edward IV was the first king to lose his throne, but then successfully invade England and win it back in battle. The tales of these two kings are symptomatic of the death throes of the medieval era.

95. Not All Comets Were Feared as Portents of Doom

In early January 1472 John Warkworth, a London citizen who kept a chronicle for over a decade, recorded amidst the great happenings of his time the passage of a comet. There is no evidence in his detailed and overtly fascinated account to suggest that either he or anyone he knew considered the appearance of this ball of fire in the sky to be a warning of impending doom.

Astronomy was in its infancy when this comet arrived. The first telescope was still a century away, but plenty of people recorded the passage of the phenomenon and many studied it as best they could, recording their findings and calculations.

In Germany, mathematician Johannes Regiomontanus made a detailed study of the comet and its movement, his treatise, *De Cometis*, becoming a bestseller as the printing press made it available far and wide. Regiomontanus tracked the comet's movement through the astrological constellations of the zodiac, noting that it moved more slowly at the beginning and end of its appearance and much faster in the middle, moving through four zodiac signs – from the end of Virgo into Gemini – in just one day. He believed that its movement described a portion of a circle, demonstrating an understanding of the elliptical orbit of comets.

The comet's tail fascinated onlookers. Regiomontanus concluded that it was orientated towards the stars of Gemini as it appeared to move from extending west to extending east, on some occasions pointing south. Angelo Cato de Supino, an Italian philosopher, recorded that the comet was as bright as the full moon and that the tail was over thirty degrees long. The passage of the comet was also recorded in Korea and China, where it was described as a 'broom star'. In all, it was recorded in its passage for fifty-nine days.

In London, John Warkworth also recorded the four-week passage of the comet as it could be seen from England. He too noted that the tail moved around. There is no trace of fear in his description of the 'white flame of fire' passing overhead from east to west, disappearing from his view on 20 February. He wrote that 'some men said that the blazings of the said star was a mile length'. Such estimates, along with those of Regiomontanus and others, were way off the mark, but were only the symptom of an early lack of scientific knowledge. The fact that it was plainly understood that this was an object of some kind, distant in the sky, travelling in an elliptical orbit and simply passing the Earth by is clear. It was watched with interest, not with fear.

96. WILLIAM CAXTON SET UP THE FIRST PRINTING PRESS IN ENGLAND

It is easy to underestimate the seismic impact of the printing press on the medieval world. Books had always been the carefully guarded right of the wealthy or the learned. Their words were in Latin, or perhaps French or Italian. As handwritten pieces of art, their cost was beyond the reach of the common man. The printing press changed all of that, making printed works affordable, able to be mass-produced and easily disseminated and reprinted. If any one item was the dawn light of a new age, it was surely the printing press.

William Caxton was born in Kent in the early 1420s, making his way to London in search of a trade and to make his fortune in 1438, when he became apprentice to Robert Large. When his master died in 1441, William moved abroad to Bruges, the focus of England's vast wool trade on the Continent. In 1463 William was appointed Governor of the English Nation of Merchant Adventurers, a position every bit as prestigious as it sounds.

During 1470, as turmoil gripped England and the Wars of the Roses blossomed once more, Caxton entered the service of Margaret, Duchess of Burgundy, sister to Edward IV. An interest in literature bloomed and Caxton began translating. He complained in a later work that handwriting meant his 'pen became worn, his hand weary, his eyes dimmed'. Caxton therefore invested some of his fortune in learning the new techniques of printing in Cologne between 1470 and 1472.

Returning to Bruges, Caxton set up his own press

along with Colard Mansion. There, Caxton printed the first book in the English language, his own translation from French entitled *The Recuyell of the Histories of Troye*. In 1476, with the political situation in England more settled and Edward IV's court gaining a reputation for Burgundian style and tastes, Caxton returned to England and set up the country's first printing press in Westminster. It was a sensational hit.

The first dated book to be printed in English was Anthony Woodville, Earl Rivers' translation of *Dictes and Sayenges of the Phylosophers* in 1476. Chaucer's *Canterbury Tales*, *The Myrrour of the World* (the first illustrated book in English), *The Game and Playe of the Chesse* and Sir Arthur Malory's *Le Morte D'Arthur* were amongst Caxton's early printing works as the new invention took England by storm.

During his lifetime Caxton produced around 100 different titles for his noble patrons. The advantages of the press soon became increasingly evident. Words and ideas could be spread further and faster than ever before, mass-produced in the language of the people. If ever there was a beacon of empowerment that might light the way to revolution, leaving the medieval period in its shadow, it was surely the printing press.

97. The First Recorded Valentine Letter in English Was Sent in 1477

The Paston Letters provide a rich vein of insight into fifteenth-century life. The Norfolk family preserved all of their correspondence, covering family matters, legal wrangles and the great events of their time. Amongst the collection of papers are several letters written in February 1477 by Marjory Brews to John Paston. They were in the process of arranging their marriage and Marjory writes excitedly to 'my right well-beloved Valentine'. These letters are the earliest surviving Valentine letters in the English language.

Marjory's mother wrote to John a few days before 14 February to invite him to visit for the weekend and discuss the marriage with Marjory's father. She asked him if he would like to visit from Thursday until Monday, as 'upon Friday is Saint Valentine's Day'. Perhaps aware that the negotiations were taking longer than might be ideal, Elizabeth Brews counselled her future son-in-law to be patient, telling him, 'It is but a simple oak, that is cut down at the first stroke.'

The next letter was written by Marjory herself informing John that her mother had been working on her father to try and improve the dowry, but to no avail. Marjory hopes that John will not be driven from the match by the apparently unsatisfactory settlement, signing her letter 'at Topcroft, with full heavy heart'.

In a third letter Marjory wrote again to her 'Right worshipful and well-beloved Valentine' to explain that she had been unable to induce her father to increase her dowry but she hoped that John would still marry her. The exchange is sweet but mingles business with the first known Valentine letter.

98. Berwick-upon-Tweed Was the Most Disputed Town in Britain

At the very edge of the Anglo-Saxon kingdom of Northumberland stood a small town. Berwick, an old Anglo-Saxon word meaning 'corn farm', was lost to the kingdom of Scotland at the Battle of Carham in 1016 and from that time onward it would become the most hotly disputed piece of land in Britain. Legend states that when the Devil was showing God all of the kingdoms of the earth he hid Berwick under his thumb so that he could keep it for himself.

When the Scottish king William the Lion attempted to invade England he was captured and Berwick was returned to England in 1174 as part of his ransom. Shortly afterwards, Richard I sold Berwick back to Scotland in an effort to raise funds for his Crusade plans. Edward I installed himself at Berwick to provide his arbitration in the matter of the Scottish succession and when war ensued, Edward took Berwick again.

In the early fourteenth century Berwick came under frequent siege by Scottish forces and it was recaptured in 1318, only for Edward III to seize it back following the Battle of Halidon Hill in 1333. The town remained disputed territory, but prospered due to its location at the border and on the River Tweed. Berwick became a centre of trade in spite of the bitter dispute over its ownership.

As the Lancastrian cause faltered in 1461 during the Wars of the Roses, Henry VI's queen, Margaret of Anjou, escaped from Wales and sailed to Scotland, where she offered control of Berwick as payment for the provision of a Scottish army to invade England with her. Peace between the two nations was still strained as the Yorkist dynasty took over England. Peace ended in 1482 when an English army, led by Richard, Duke of Gloucester (later Richard III), marched to Berwick and on to Edinburgh. Berwick-upon-Tweed fell under siege and has remained an English town ever since.

Disputed for centuries, Berwick-upon-Tweed has both an English and a Scottish identity and has belonged to both nations at different times. It provided its owner with a platform to launch raids into the other country and control of lucrative trade paths. As probably the most disputed spot of land in Britain, the fight for control of Berwick is a microcosm of the rifts that have tormented the British Isles across the centuries, until peace between the nations was finally achieved.

99. Richard III Did Not Steal the Throne

The fate of the two boys forever remembered as the Princes in the Tower is one of the greatest, most enduring and divisive mysteries in history. It remains a mystery because there is no evidence to provide certainty as to the fate of Edward V and his brother Richard, Duke of York.

The spring and summer of 1483 are shrouded in mist and confusion that cannot be made sense of at this distance. Much of the interpretation of events is subjective, driven for a long time by the image of Richard III crafted by William Shakespeare. The discovery and identification of the remains of Richard III in Leicester have done little to resolve the controversy that still surrounds a man who was only king for just over two years.

Edward IV died on 9 April 1483. His oldest son, Edward, was at Ludlow with his maternal uncle Anthony Woodville, Earl Rivers. The twelve-year-old prince was proclaimed king, and his paternal uncle, Richard, Duke of Gloucester, met the new king's entourage near Northampton. However, Richard had been warned by Edward IV's close friend Lord Hastings that the Woodvilles were plotting against him.

Richard took possession of the young king and imprisoned Anthony, along with one of the king's half-brothers and other members of his household. When they arrived in London preparations were made for the coronation and almost everyone seemed content. The former queen had taken her other son and her daughters into sanctuary at Westminster Abbey, fearful of Richard's intentions.

As preparations for the coronation continued, Richard was confirmed as Protector of the Realm in accordance with his brother's will. He pressurised the former queen, Elizabeth Woodville, into handing over her other son to keep the young king company and so that he could attend his brother's coronation.

Within days a sermon was preached alleging that Edward IV's marriage was illegitimate, a charge that was soon dropped, and that his marriage had been bigamous, making his children illegitimate and unable to succeed. This made Richard the lawful heir and he was petitioned to take the throne.

Edward V and his brother ceased to be seen in the grounds of the Tower, leading to rumours of their murder. There was never anything more than rumour and conjecture though. To many, Richard III remains a ruthless and ambitious man who wanted the throne and removed every obstacle in his path.

Richard III did not kill his nephews in order to take the crown. They were seen for weeks after he was crowned on 6 July 1483. If he killed them it was to remove them as figureheads for rebellions that were growing in their name, but which would eventually adopt Henry Tudor as a figurehead. There are other candidates for their murderers and even theories that they survived. Without new evidence, it will remain a mystery and a well-spring of controversy.

100. Henry Tudor's Invasion Brought a New Dynasty, but Not a New Era

Since 1066 there had been several significant invasions of England, most notably by Prince Louis of France in 1216. Throughout the Hundred Years Wars in the fourteenth century there had been incessant raids on the South Coast of England that may not qualify as invasions, but which certainly saw foreign troops in action against English troops on English soil. The landing of Henry Tudor at Milford Haven in Wales on 7 August 1485 led directly to the Battle of Bosworth on 22 August, a point in history frequently but arbitrarily used to mark the end of the medieval period.

Henry Tudor had lived in exile, firstly in Brittany and latterly in France, for the last fourteen of his twenty-eight years – half his life. His invasion was backed and funded by the French crown, keen to see the martially minded Richard III distracted from any plans to invade France. Tudor was nominally the Earl of Richmond, the title of his father Edmund Tudor, who had died before Henry was born. Natural Lancastrians during the Wars of the Roses, Henry's family had lost everything. He had been joined in his exile by his devoted uncle, Jasper Tudor, Earl of Pembroke.

When Henry landed at Mill Bay he had around 2,000 men in his army, almost all French mercenaries and criminals provided by the King of France. His numbers were swollen during his march through Wales and when he met Richard III at the Battle of Bosworth he won a monumental victory, transformed from exile to king by his French-backed invasion.

The beginning of the Tudor era, and therefore the date of the Battle of Bosworth, is viewed as the end of the medieval era and the beginning of the early modern period. Whilst it is convenient to nominate a specific date, the truth is far less clearly defined. As a man who had lived his adult life in exile and had no experience or training for power, Henry VII fell back on many of the Yorkist institutions of government that Edward IV had used, such as the chamber system of finance and the practise of installing an heir at Ludlow to govern the Marches as Prince of Wales. Early Tudor government was a continuation of what had gone before rather than a revolution.

Henry Tudor's was not the final invasion of the period either, though it was the only successful regime change. Over the next decade both Lambert Simnell and Perkin Warbeck would try to unseat the infant Tudor regime. The end of the medieval era did not arrive with Henry Tudor's French mercenaries. It was born during the reign of Edward IV and matured while Henry VIII occupied the throne his father had won, driven as much by changes in the rest of the world as by political developments in Britain.

Also available from Amberley Publishing

THE STUARTS IN 100 FACTS

ANDREA ZUVICH